Where Have All the Hippies Gone

by

Nina Keller

Dedication

To Differences, to Trust and to Friends, may I get this published before you leave this plane, and to Judy Gugajew Finestone and Suzy who have. To Roy at 97, who taught me to challenge authority and who did not ascribe to pride but said, "I've thought of it further and there is one thing I am proud of. My family is diverse like the UN." And to Floss Carpenter, a most generous, inclusive, non-judgemental role model, a generational anomaly.

Appreciations

Rob Cox U MA Special Collections
>   where many farm activists have their documents
>   stored
>   where my father's photos, (Roy Finestone) are
>   collected for viewing

Country Joe for Viet Nam Experience, lyrics, vocals, politics
>   and his anti-Viet Nam

"Fixin to Die Rag"

Frank Zappa "Without deviation from the norm, progress is
>   not possible."

Emily Dickinson "How strange that nature does not knock
>   and yet does not intrude."

For generosity of editing time:

Hedy Tripp, reader of rough draft, lover of story, history,
>   herstory

John Abrams, unstinting with time and bounteous with
>   commodity, a writer

Pam Richardson, incisive Wendell historian

Caleb Keller, an astute proof reader

Betsy Corner, an inspiration, mover and groover

Paul Richmond big-hearted publisher, IT support and for
>   loving Suzy

Richard Finestone and Blanche James, sibs, for showing
>   deeper interest

Shoshanna Rhine and Marty Jezer for pointing out that no
>   matter how hurtful a critique may be, one can pluck
>   from it, one shred of truth

Verandah Porche "When love unravels, self-improvement is
>   so easy."

Gerry Feil for recognizing and filming the wonder of hippie
>   lives

Bob Dylan, our bard

For Respect, Compassion, Kindness and Honesty

-----

[1] U MA Archives/Rob Cox Special Collections/photographs/Famous
Long Ago/Roy Finestone

Published by Human Error Publishing
www.humanerrorpublishing.com
paul@humanerrorpublishing.com

Copyright © 2025
by
Human Error Publishing
Nina Keller

ISBN: 978-1-948521-26-0

Cover photo C E Green

All other photos by Roy Finestone and Sue Kramer

CHAPTERS

PHILADELPHIA

LEAVING PHILADELPHIA

FIRST SIGHTINGS of the Johnson Pasture aka The Baby Farm

TO MONTAGUE

Origins

This account responds to why in the 60's there were major upheavals, different from and more widespread from prior generations. There was desperation about Jim Crow and resistance to the military draft. My friends knew the Viet Nam war was illegitimate. Knowing and acting upon beliefs is quite different. I was a typical immature white woman who unpredictably matured and fortuitously was introduced to direction and self-esteem.

We attach to stories of passion, survival and beating the odds. In 1969, when I was 23, I was attracted to rebellion but did not know much about choosing my way. I was a "slow" learner. I followed protocol until it distorted and broke me. I left a wonderful person I should never have married. No one ever modeled how to resist a marriage proposal. I submitted. Was I weak or typical?

Until focus redirects within, it is on others. That was the way of women in movies, in literature, in my family, in this country and the world.

Take care of others.

Be a teacher, a nurse, a secretary.

Make a home. Have kids.

In conjunction with that, identities strove to be expressed.

Reject insignificant thinking.

Protest what's wrong.

Be different from the crowd.

Are you misunderstood? Alone and incomplete. Are you wrong? Nah! These are inconveniences.

But then, a twig snaps. Look out! It's a bear, a stalker. It's a twig.

Chase a pack of wild coyotes in your night clothes. They want to devour your flock, your precious kitty and then you. If you laid down long enough, the chickens would consume you.

Just be brave.

But how?

At my 50th high school reunion someone told me how cool I was back then. What? I was not cool at all. That perception revealed expansive youthful floundering. The impressive Salt Lake City author, Terry Tempest Williams advised how to stop an attacking bear. If you bare your breasts when all else fails, then you may deflect the bear's resentment because of its unwavering respect for mother. She investigated a spectrum between succumbing to fear or choosing courage.

A spectrum is a long avenue of coils. We may not know we are courageous until we reflect upon our actions. Was our exploit consciously decisive or instinctual? Sometimes courage happens to you. There is no explanation for those who do not react courageously. Advice does not always work. Some hearts hurt too deeply so bravery may not be an option. How does optimism sprout? From love, from mom, from a fish on a line, from eggs in the nest, from an adequate back scratcher, from an abandoned shack, from birth, from recognizing potential?

Grandmom Rebecca, fleeing European antisemitism, immigrated to Philadelphia, PA, recognized indications of the failing economy. Every Shabbos the day of rest, and as a well deserving mother of eight, she put her swollen feet up, listened to the opera and read the paper. She knew, she read, she listened and she understood. "Morris, get our money out of the bank!" "Nah! This is America." After The Crash forced foreclosure on Grandpa's copper smelter shop, they devised a plan. He constructed a mobile cart fueled with Grandma's Friday fish cakes and rolled it into the subway which delivered him to the Catholic fish-eating neighborhoods. Later when Dad went off to war in Japan, my mother, pregnant with her second child, me, knew how to cope courageously for she was her mother's daughter. There was no choice but to be privately fearful, for thousands of wives shared her dread. Dad returned whole plus surplus Nagasaki radioactivity near his brain. (Benign!)

Why did a suburban middle child leave all behind, her happy family, her small but precious record collection, and take to the road? Loving my family was not enough. I had them for considerable time without being further inspired. I needed different people and to actively reject bourgeois values. My definition of bourgeoisie is someone who buys whatever they want. Ever hear of Reverend Billy and "The Stop Shopping Chorus"?

Rebellion was tangible, an undermining of traditions that were once solid. My 10th grade English teacher, Mr. Schuster, opened that door of possibility. He was semi Bohemian, he did work regular hours, but he was not crisp, a somewhat attractive shag in his perennial tweed with gratuitous worn leather elbow patches. He was not a laborious operative having us copy for copy sake. He'd secured a privileged and smoky side room where there were suggestions of alternatives to conformity where authority was casually flaunted with his elite cast of lit-magazine characters. He wrote disturbing off color poetry, dashed in on the other side of the late bell, leapt on his desk and passionately recited Shakespeare.

Bohemian literature pulsed. Despicable Viet Nam war drummed, civil rights were stripped, murder of activists was persistent, Nazis were real, how to respond meaningfully was vague, smoking dope changed perspective. Because of the glory of my Janis Joplin hair, my musician brother fantasized my singing in his band. I had not been a singer since strumming the auto-harp in elementary school. Singing was not my call. Carefree beatnik style was embryonic; hair and clothes a façade for I had not yet reasoned how to coalesce personal distinction with resistance against what gushed haywire.

Dashingly bad Americana had shackled us, from the simplest to the most profound dictums: prioritize financial success, amass possessions, embrace formalities of mar-riage, discard outdated possessions, cross at corners, wear a watch, knot your tie, get married first, don't speak out, go to college, pay for war, go to war, ignore poverty, pray, shut up, the men will protect you, and horribly subverting, believe that the powers that be are so powerful it does not matter if you protest. These admonishing perverse absur-dities repelled, while the 60's prairie-fired[1] passionately. Shred the ties, the bra and certainly, Burn the Draft Card. The criminality of Viet Nam hemorrhaged into the streets. We aspired to discover and develop our own laws.

Do you resist the Nazis, the Russian military? Do you get shot immediately or flee to the forest, discover yourself, accept what confronting yourself reveals, and find courage? The underground is on the only dirt road you have ever traveled. If it takes you into the deep south at the end of which is a speak easy and you are the only white person in sight, stand up my sister. It's time to move!

---

1 Theme and motto of The Weather Underground was, "One spark, ten thousand sparks, prairie fire!"

Prelude to the Wild

There was privilege and minor luxury in my rebellion. I had a car and a small savings. Those who were unable to separate from home, carried on rebellion where they lived. Others donned external symbols of rebellion, long hair, no bra, patched clothes. But political rebellion was rooted unquenchably deeper. Because young people en mass were craving release from traditional restrictions, a magnetic vortex was generated.

Charismatic leadership and violence were prevalent. Our national conscience was rocked to action by MLK's electrifying eloquence and leadership, civil rights worker's courage, voter registration and murder of activists, The Weather Underground,[2] The Venceramos Brigades finding their way to Cuba to help with harvest, The Black Panthers' assertive identity and resistance to racism, Black Power as pride, Malcolm X's passionate oratorical evolution from miscegenation to embracing other races, the complications of his murder, confrontation with sexism, the underground press, back to the land and Thoreauvian simplicity and farming. There was outrage about the judicial mistreatment of The Chicago Seven. The day after their trial, we wore T D A buttons (The Day After) and felt exhilaration for Ed Abbey who could envision the destruction of the Grand Coulee Dam on the Columbia River in WA[3] as positive environmental response, if not necessity.

Music and antics of resistance thrilled, Bob Dylan vowed "forever young," Nina Simone reminded us how her soul was occupied with history and "Pirate Jenny," Woodstock was free and splattered with mud, jazz reflected internal combustion and the Blues vocalized hard times. We went *On the Road* with Jack Kerouac, protested against the war machine of all our presidents. Jim Crow and

---

2   The Weather Underground, a radical militant offshoot of Students for a Democratic Society, SDS, originally The Weathermen, staging actions against the government and its wars tactics
"You don't need a weatherman to know which way the wind blows..."
Bob Dylan song "Subterranean Homesick Blues"
3   The Monkey Wrench Gang, Ed Abbey 1975 novel about environmental sabotage

innumerable lynchings revolted us and compelled risky response – the Montgomery Bus Boycott, police beatings of peaceful protesters at the Edmund Pettus Bridge, restaurant counter sit-ins, Black youth en masse being recognized. Isn't that enough? What do I overlook?

My father had been highly sensitized to social injustices. He had toyed with radical rhetoric, attended a few "meetings," and desired political exchange. "So kids, every night one of us will bring an article of interest to discuss." That was a good idea but lacking adequate professorial skill, his inspiration fell wearily away. He needed sophisticated exchange after hours at his accountant's desk rather than summonsing the energy to direct childish exploration. Instead, he taught us to challenge authority.

Where do young people go to find their place? The national pandemonium activated my decision to leave Philadelphia. I had been an inner city junior high teacher married to an artist I loved. I was not in love. I did not recognize the difference between types of love. Social pressures influenced twenty-one-year young me, feminist advice was unfamiliar and alternatives were vague.

Broad and Olney was a visually familiar North Philadelphia neighborhood, familiar only during my college years en route to Temple University. The 55 Bus with subway transfer had deposited me there twice daily. Years of riding public transportation was an influential part of my college education. During that two hour dose in transit, I more attentively investigated faces, the fascinating theater of differences, than college texts on trigonometry or the hierarchy of European royalty.

Like typical public transportation riders, I devoured fat pretzels and bulbous chestnuts from trees not yet decimated by blight. Stiff faced vendors peddled from fire fueled push carts and defrosted their fingers with each scoop and sale. This neighborhood was where my rocky initiation into teaching at the junior high level had begun. I recognized the solid potential of brick and stone row homes as they had initially been constructed. Now, empty store fronts and decaying structures, trash, and chaos dominated the main drag. The positive role models sheltered their families behind locked yet breachable sanctuaries. This deteriorating area was somebody's neighborhood, good people who kept rollin' in memories and hope. Talent and its germination were hard for outsiders to see.

One late broiling evening, in trying to maneuver our car past rough street throngs of night people out for a breath of something, the sad demise of another working class neighborhood was evident and typically American. Faces leered into the relative safety of our car and fists pounded our hood. The barrier between us and absorption was thin. The lock button was up. I felt guilty pushing it down in the face of a black apparition. He was a real man blurred by decay and fury. He was livid with something white and tangible to ram, easier to confront than systems of neglect and racism.

Courage, I wonder? Courage can be invisible and unrecorded. There are the brave living in ghettos with overwhelming odds.

Fifty years later, that poverty and chaos live on. If I had stayed urban, my attentions would have been confronted and redirected.

"You care more for others than you do for your own people," my sister challenged. That was not accurate. The history of my Jewish clan roots deeply in my identity. I consciously relate to the problems of others because of inherited values beyond personal needs.

Friends sat on the rug, the joint was passed. We whirled in the high. A French acquaintance had just exited with his flamboyant pet, an ocelot. Another friend entered with an appendage on his back which he tenderly lowered to the floor. It was the living torso of a Viet Nam victim here in this country for prosthetic attentions. This human then sat propped with us and sucked madly at the illegal smoldering release; his agony became ours. How logical that the bearer of that human weight became extreme in his underground rebellion against the government. My dismayed father re-layed an account about that friend who said, "If I didn't think I could change the world, I'd kill myself!"

I was nagged by ineffectual response to injustice so I left city life to seek direction beyond my own aura. It was by eventually belonging to a community of activists, that the political spectrum and reasoning sophisticated. I became active within the Montague Farm community, one of three sister farm communes in the CT River Valley. Role modeling and experimenting with community fomented resistance to war and the anti-nuclear movement.[4]

Sam Lovejoy toppled a utility weather tower (1975) as an act of civil disobedience to protest the construction of two nuclear reactors on the Montague Plains. His controversial act became national news. I received *Osawatame*, a Weather Underground publication wrapped discretely in brown paper from sources unknown. My friend Ron, a mainstay in the Weather Underground, later reconsidered an earlier opinion regarding the environmental movement as frivolous privilege as opposed to the necessity of radical social rebellion. The connections between political foes whether military/industrial, environmental or corporate was evident. We did stop two reactors by the way.[5]

A question remains: We uniformly are subjects of the same sickened planet. How can they not commit to global health? We are not the only ones who have offspring. Crying hurts too deeply. Put it over there on the shelf. No! Put it behind the plant. Bring pain out once in a while and return it in good time. How big is the loss? Is it rape, fire, murder, the loss of a child?

"You never get over the loss of a child," my mother-in-law revealed. "You learn to carry on." This account is how we do very well enough, with moving on.

---

4   Stephen Diamond's *What the Trees Said*, Ray Mungo's *Famous Long Ago*, many GMP Documentary Films, the local Rowe, Vermont Yankee and Seabrook Nukes, civil disobedience, Anna Gyorgy's *NO NUKES*, Harvey Wasserman's *History of the United States*, The Muse Concerts in NY City

5   *Lovejoy's Nuclear War* GMP Films

Leaving Philadelphia

Stumbling upon Communes

How exhilarating it had been to be in my first apartment in the mixed neighborhood of Germantown, Philadelphia, especially after the monochrome of suburbia. But circumstances in 1969 had me on the move. The bare rental mattress showed wear. I lay in that rented space and waited for dawn to direct me north into New England to "find land" and "to grow our own." Graffiti broadcast "JARVO, POSH AND BIGGIE" a trio I never knew. My triangle was with two friends, one who wanted to be alone from me and the other only with me, and me, in the fruitless triangle of sheer stymied desire. The vector of direction willowed in my side view mirror. Goodbye Philly and hello to what came next.

We three had been rigorously experimenting for a year with righteous Michio Kushi's Japanese diet called macrobiotics which claimed strict dietary directives would lead to spiritual well-being and ph health. Brown rice and seaweed. "Calm down! It's pretty good after all," was mid-scale on the ph balance and was called a #7 diet. Balancing acid/yin, and alkalinity/yang would avoid the disease spectrum. The extremes of triple yin like vinegar, sugar, tomatoes, eggplant, peppers, dairy and triple yang being meat were taboo. We enjoyed simplicity, embraced austerity and believed in the guiding regimen. In the faculty room, the teachers poked elbows at my homemade rice balls and chewed without pulverizing their fried tidbits.

We traveled together until the crossroads at Black Ruby's cabin where we diverged. Ruby, a more experienced macro adherent prepared buckwheat, green pepper and onion smothered in sharp cheddar. She remonstrated that for balance, austerity could in reverse fashion, skew one's personality. Did Michio Kushi, the macrobiotic guru, not smoke tobacco?

I departed into the Green Mountains to find Pam Ransom, my city friend who had relocated to an early Vermont commune. Pam was looking for a place to have her baby, rather than with the father, Woody at his Bryn Athyn, or its breakaway, Rock Bottom Farm.[6] There I met warm and welcoming Martha Heller. Communal enterprise was not evident and pleasurable anarchy seemed to reign with swimming, beer run, chips and an all providing sense of love. The kitchen presented a cold wood stove where a bare bone floated in a doggie pot. With my emerging interest in diet, I was grossly disaffected, yet generated a loaf out of "Oh look what we have here!" Corn meal and a functioning propane oven. One of Martha's children was Robbie, a youngster who lived and reputedly accomplished every function in his room on his bear skin rug. Fanfare announced he was about to launch his homemade rocket. All converged for the display, he emerged from his grotto, the mechanism fizzled and he retreated to correct malfunction.

Charles Thompson Smith was a notorious shaggy Harvard Amharic/Native American language scholar to those who knew. "Charles, you have had quite a life. You ought to write a book." "There already are tooooo many boooooks!" At mid 30's, endearing Charles, was a patriarch to a younger cadre. He lent eager embraces and his welcoming presence soon filled my VW's rear seat with un-groomed burly beard, congenial starch and agreeable commentary. For Pam's interest, we would locate the renowned Baby Farm via marks on a paper bag, as good a map as any for the out of way commune, directions to, reticent neighbors could reveal, and didn't want to. "Oh ho! Turn around if you want to go forward. Everything depends if you are north of the border."

---

6   Pam eventually reconciled with Woody and had further births at his dairy farm, Bryn Athyn.

The JP aka The Baby Farm, an ironic title

The JP or Johnson Pastures, received its duplicate name, "The Baby Farm," after Michael and Annie Carpenter's early commune home birth of Red Pony. Michael had humbly inherited a small sum from the military, after his father's death, enough to place a down payment on the off the grid acreage. The Carpenters embraced high ideals. They were the first non Natives I heard ascribe to not being owners of land they owned. "This land belongs to itself, or god or all people." I did not know of the history of the Johnson people, only their being ancestors of those who had moved away.

Charles, Pam and I parked at the beginning of the unmarked dirt road. The road boasted the glue of boulders, rugged enemy to oil pans. There were no identifying signs other than tire grooves. We proceeded skeptically about a mile before seeing anyone, no houses or wires or sounds of human exchange. It was not the JP we encountered. It was a consortium of The Brotherhood of the Spirit[7] relocated from their prior Leyden habitation, a potato barn, to share the Carpenter's largess until they could be settled on their own. They constructed basic lodgings and a carpentry feat of a three-tiered tree house of whimsical architectural delight.[8]

"Come back and stay with us. The Baby Farm is over the hill."

After I moved to the JP and met Michael Carpenter, I called the era the saga of The Michaels. Michael Carpenter and Michael Metelica would sometime meet and JP Michael

---

7   *Brotherhood of the Spirit* Documentary. ca.1973. Group book, *The Spirit of the Brotherhood*

8   Some members of The Brotherhood remain in this valley with generous community spirit, optimism, political resistance. Annie Hassett with her powerful vocals can play guitar and sing songs of resistance tirelessly. Cheech, photography/massage, Brian McCue is renowned wizardly master- carpenter. Laurel Lussen, graceful banter, bright, beautiful and educated. Eddie Munster as I called him, was the kind giant. Dale Sluter, craftsman carpenter, remains a friendly elder with long reddish hair and father of my later high school student, fire juggler and hula hoop artist. Elana, mother of two commune kids and my darling high school students, Renny and Nina.

would return with a special hum of private business but no small talk. Michael Metelica, The Brotherhood commune leader and progeny of Elwood Babbitt, trans medium, would energize, spiritualize and eventually disappoint the Brotherhood's hundreds of diverse members by diverging from community and healthy living. He reputedly could read your aura. "Just lie down and take off your clothes," one member told me. Their youthful camaraderie and optimism were appealing but there were too many gauzy eyes!

FIRST SIGHTINGS

The geographical roll of mounded Vermont hills made pleasant viewing. Laborers had preceded us by generations, had hewn and eyeballed where forest would be tamed and receded to provide access and solar gain. Field and pasture were the mainstay of white man's agricultural endeavor. Push the trees back. Plow, plant, grow and encourage with blood, sweat and yes, tears.

We ambled over the knoll away from the guru lovers to locate the Baby Farm, The Pastures, due to its former status among the encroaching forests, those ineluctable forces which reclaim abandoned fields. It had been years since cows had grazed, so brambles and goldenrod redoubled in force. It was mostly a tract of forested acreage but an open space, the erstwhile pasture, remained visible in a wild state revealing the shape of a hillside upon which people mingled. We were invited to join a collection of youths without obvious goals, some tending a fire, some enjoying the liberty of scant clothing and the company of too many unruly dogs.

Why a pasture far off a main road? This is not an unresolved matter. The historical answer was economics. Animal husbandry and development of pasture land led shepherds and herders to move drove and flock to accessible property. With a willingness to careen with earth, farmers moved onto affordable land where they could find it. Prime land had been devoured and second comers moved further from rich river bottom grasses to rockier climes where animals worked hard to subsist on various growth. Seeds blew in. Grasses migrated. Off the beaten track, old timers conveniently constructed homes sensibly abutting the slender horse trail. In decades, houses were subject to roar and discharge through garden and front door when roads were widened and paved.

Currently it was disposition that led home owners to relocate farther out of town. Seeking greenery, privacy, silence, escape from traffic, exchange with beast, bird, water, wind and sky. How precious absolute darkness that then reveals the firmament.

Remains of a dwelling were not recognizable to the untrained eye or perhaps none had dotted that landscape. It was green and brown and green all over except where people had invaded which forced mud and briar. Expert foresters can read landscape,[9] identify primary, secondary and tertiary growth where forest had been clear cut. What I was able to see was directed towards signs of human habitation, the center of which, the core of comfort and offering, was the camp fire.

In the distinction between hippies, some were individualized, not relying on shallow baubles and head bands although the attachment to flowers and beads did express hippie alignment with nature and Natives. Some hippies were older, some clever, educated and skilled. But there was conformity in the masses of sixties fever as in any cross section of people. Not all were dropping out. Some were dropping into. True friends were in the making. The World was expansive and ablaze with possibility.

The JP was a miracle of place with its rough frame kitchen lean-to near the potable stream, tents, a tipi, a slit trench, a rough board shack and dissimilar long-haired characters.

In one year, Chuck, my eventual partner, tallied hash marks of 800 visitors come to soak up our wilderness, initiative and broth. These parade faces were reflective of the times, people seeking logic, belonging, excitement or photo opportunity. We claimed pages in sociology textbooks. A photo of us, yes, it's us, a frontispiece for a paragraph on alternative families. Suburbia had no charm and the city had lost its draw. Many were seeking meaning to life, wresting free onto dirt road offerings. We became young carpenters proud on a first high beam, hammering elemental nails into surety. There were no sidewalk cracks to count. No spoons to set straight or toilet to swab.

9   *Reading the Forested Landscape* Tom Wessels 1999

The cook lean-to was replete with implements, standard hippie bulk food (rice, beans, oatmeal, tamari, miso, whole wheat flour) and basic tools. Under the sky, a crude circular wooden table expressed cyclical themes of nature and registered equality for the diners with no leader at the head of a table. A giant pot of harvested apricots or plums simmered sweetly over the open fire pit which sparked and smoldered because of green wood. California Phil stirred the brew with his Bowie knife, a dramatic useful identifying trait, the leather sheath hung strapped from his hip. Various newfound kin wandered about the hills in loin cloths and jeans, relieved to have so passed the day in partnership with nature, in whose bosom they nearly dwelled.

A few rules were consensually agreed upon by suggestion of the young and respected Carpenter landowners. There were strong moments of clarity months before the communal train wreck. The owners returned intermittently to gain mortal perspective on the caretaking of land. "We can't live here full time so we won't tell you what to do. We suggest these rules... Anyone can live here. This is God's land. People don't own land. No one is turned away... Those who live here will figure out how to do things. There are no rules of ownership, no compulsory pooling of funds, no leaders, gurus or bosses. Give what you like and take what you need."

The rules were:

no runaways

no minors w/o parental permission

no drugs or alcohol

no soap or shitting in the stream.

We were early environmentalists.

The Vermont hills rang with space and freedom.

We were choosing to live without running water and electricity. Some city relatives advised from their second home beach houses that I receive psychiatric attention while we reveled in peaceful darkness. To their faithless eyes, I was regressing into childhood. They wanted me to prove myself "under God" while they godlessly challenged hardy and deep pleasures of self-sufficiency free from the electric switch.

"How can you stand to live with so many people. There's no privacy!"

"We have the forests. And, an airy outhouse!"

The camp fire picked two animated males from the dark. Chuck and Fritz. Their appearance had not surprised me. How could it? I was the visitor, they the residents.

Chuck and Fritz were returning home, the fledgling country boy, an escapee from Long Island and the smooth judge's son. They had been down to the Henry Farm to help with haying and had brought home lovely samples stuck most noticeably in one's golden ravages of hair. The dry grass stems and bits were everywhere. Reaching uninhibitedly into crevices to dislodge or to pleasure himself, one made a point that manners were obviously a thing of the past.

Chuck was unruly wild, his "overhauls" fashioned by a girlfriend from an American flag. I could view his chest and on down towards regions beyond and I wondered whether the farm hands had taken such liberties? What was visible was public, and public art, pubic art, was aired. He had not given a glance my way. I was less than insignificant. He insinuated and smirked, yet the two young men possessed the audience and me, the newcomer. They laughed revealing beautiful as yet unstained teeth. Chuck's insolent lip curled. He was magnetic but I was repelled; I was lured by his muscular body, his adult cynicism.

Juicy lips smacked at the preserves California Phil stirred like alchemy over the cauldron fire and then lathered luxuriously like starving children, on the NY city bagel from a bottomless brown bag Chuck's committed father, Mike, had gifted. It was indicative of Mike that he had driven arduously in pursuit of his son. Mike later told me that before real estate, he had been a long-distance truck driver. He loved to travel the country, his bronzed elbow propped on the open window, his fateful cigarette poised in what could be distinct to truckers' relaxation on the highway. I looked askance at the white bread, not quite triple yin or triple yang, but off the macrobiotic scale of acceptable.

I had baked a travel loaf of solid brown rice bread. Someone spread mustard on the scant remains of my offering. "See ye not all these things. Be not deceived. Many false prophets shall arise!"[10] I joined the fire pit circle where the two golden boys, although one of them was shaved down to a handsomely shaped scalp where fuzz sprouted, were the best show for the attention they garnered.

What is this place? A foreign planet! The woman with the omnipresent baby on her hip and no diaper, tee hee, some pee, hippies in loin cloths, some serious, some lighthearted, wandered down from the hills to the ring of the dinner triangle or Michael calling the collection of us to "STEAM BATH." His melodious voice and harmonium resonated mellow echoes in the hills. He had directed the construction of poles pulled down to arcing, tied and covered with old rugs and whatnot, a small entryway to bucket in fired rocks to be placed in the central pit. Water sprinkled produced the resultant steam, the higher one sat the hotter, hot enough to scald or blister, we were so tough. Let me out of here! And the plunk into the shallow stream good enough to succor. I recognized wonderful people, some of whom are dear today. I had to stay.

Passion suits youth. Being a hippy suggested that sex was not only accessible and free, but also easy. This fantastic distinction generated a misleading yet pervasive taunt. Reputedly being sex, drugs, rock and roll dignitaries, did not mean we were expert. Most of us experimented. Women received guys who wanted to get "it on" but balked about getting it right. Investigating someone's body is not natural for everyone. How do we learn to touch, to listen? We experience our own reactions but how obscuring and self-centered passion can be. Some of us are plain old sexy. Good at the dance. But then, not with everyone. Media unrealistically modeled machismo, receptivity, passion and simplified rejection and disappointment, but the passion of youth prevailed.

When I moved to the JP, I was invited to share a musty

_____

10   Biblical psalm

tent with Jeff, another fugitive from NY. I knew him

superficially. Do I accurately recall his name? I do recall that
he was a kind and handsome young man obsessed with the
occupation of eating just right, a triple yang burdock root diet.
He dumbfounded the neighbor, Joe Habich, whose yard
at the beginning of our dirt road proliferated with wild
burdock with its pesky Velcro burs. Joe's eyes rolled that anyone placed value in the weeds for Jeff offered to dig for the
roots. Jeff would comb for an inordinate length of time and
then more so. I thought of him as "The Mad Brush" as if
stimulus would cure a weak tendency in follicles. His hair
brush was a non-critical companion. In the dark military
green of the canvas tent I knew from the rhythmical sound,
that he was in active pursuit of salvation while he perhaps
counter productively brushed away remaining roots. He
counted the hairs keeping tally to prove his labor was
justified and therefore scientific. At a beach, we shoveled
and sculpted climb on constructions for kids whose parents
allowed them to join the "crazies." Being uninhibited on the
beach does not reflect sexual confidence. Because I shared his
sleeping bag, I cared. Premature orgasm, common enough,
left novices insecure as if it were a forever plague. He lay in-
communicado and tortured. I couldn't figure out my role with
that lovely young man. I was not the right source for illumination.
Generous Jeff offered his tent to my city parents who followed me to the ends of drivable earth in a car that
relinquished its oil pan to the road. They slept on the ground
in their own bags. Mom baked bread in the "hardly an oven"
and dad split wood. They were the courageous ones. Two days
later, I watched as they trod their way back to the car parked
at Habich's. "Your mother cried the whole way home." What
did Dad's poignancy really suggest? The
dismay of seeing their daughter re-anchored and incom-
prehensibly remote, no-phone-out-of-touch, an extreme
divergence from the envisioned path. It had been
challenging enough when I left Phila after my white dress
(knee length) back yard wedding. Mom's heart needed time to
expand. And that it gracefully did when she familiarized with,
and more so, embraced my next communal experience.

My concerns returned to Jeff. Gently, but with hurt and recrimination, I transferred to a vacated plastic tipi far up the hill before deep cold set in.

Evening solitude was so vast and the silence of sky so thick it became a new sound. Distinct animal screes and growls, nearby skittering and shuffling at night wounded and wondered my ears. Stars were undiluted by human illumination. The fragrance of the forest was inhaled where calm and patience reigned. Pupils dilated without vision inhibiting flashlights. I navigated with emergent wakefulness but was meekly aware of nocturnal animals. I learned to see with my feet.

The prickery trail threatened bare feet; more difficult was avoiding the terrible leaks. When weather hit hard, we shuttered down under tarps. Rain was formidable, loud, long and intense, until the glorious sun reappeared. Then came the drying out period when spirits rose as visibly as the evaporating damp.

While confinement on cement offered a roof, living close to the elements was a choice. The disposition of nature is to obey gravity, trickle and flow, rivulet to brook, all tributaries to the mighty river, all the way down, we say down, to lower and lowest, the mightiest sea. I responded to the magnetism and rode the tide.

Sleeping alone brought contentment. A vast expanse of unimpeded night sky opulent with stars or the artwork of clouds, represented eternal dimensions and human insignificance. As a city person I had not given attention to restricted snippets of sky.

That young girl began to feel nature like this, "Oh, then OH! A constellation, there, and there. And it will be there tomorrow and tomorrow and if the sky is clear and if vision remains, then I will see stars forever and I will be me and I will also be different for I will change as I am changing now and every moment of thought in which I think something different and do not repeat myself I will be different again and again and that moon which is mine tonight, and those leaves through which it shines down on me, down through this leaky plastic cover that only leaks light onto this dry night, those leaves will fall and lie and will grow again, sprouts will bud again as I will too, but so differently. That moon shines on everyone if they only know that is so. It shines on the world but it is mine tonight and maybe again tomorrow if I am still aware. The creatures of the night know I am here and care so little for who I am but for my smell and things I tote, residue in the laces or the soles. Who will impact tomorrow, the crooked and the straight, those who care and those who care about themselves or no one at all. I am coming alive alone here on this edge of the wild, and it is the alone that makes sure it happens."

Seasons became newly identifiable. A sliver moon indicated a new start and I observed wax and wane, ebb and flow. I was attracted to what was underfoot where I spotted waterways, soil changes, root, stem, stalk, flower, pebble, feather, ruts and ruin. The smallest piece of plastic was not innocuous and washday disclosed refuse pocketed there.

The glory of snow and ice crystals sparkled graceful arcs and shapes of trunk. Branch and twig were defined against background. White, whiter still, so the dominance of nature controlled the moment and absorbed, convinced and minimized human presence.

"It's colder over there," colder in the valley where frost settled, a reality revealed by experience. North, south, east or west exposures granted varying degrees of protection and comfort. "Rise and shine. You're under a protective hemlock. No! It's a widow maker!"[11]

"Here comes the sun."

Warm up you early riser or put yourself to bed with the heat still penetrating your western slope.

For the first time I was not seeking a partner. I had no role models.

"Who am I, what do I want, what am I good at?"

Soon I was running in the hills, feeling freedom like what a child feels. Leaping boulder to boulder, a snake coiled

---

11   Widow maker: morbid reminder that upper limbs of a tree, especially dead boughs, that receiving strong gusts of wind, may fall upon what lies beneath, crushing and so, producing a widow

and tightened on the rock below. The only animal I feared was human. I continued racing, leaping sure footed down the incline. Gutsy, I jumped in the cold stream, our untainted water source so full of intoxicating oxygen with the sweet taste that pure water has. And so clear you see through to pebbles and minnows.

We washed clothes like the ancients in the brook and scored a 12" diameter clothes washer that cranke on an axis. Did we call it Herbie? Squish in one pair of jeans, a smidgeon of soap, some water. Oh how lovely outside life was in mountain air. Carry water buckets to fill an outdoor bathtub, light a fire beneath and soak under the sky. If someone was resourceful, any furniture, carpet or item furnished our space. We were stepping up, out of emptiness into hand-me-down comfort. Happy we were. So many children playing at life. Like cowboys we casually rolled our own cigarettes from the cans of Bugler tobacco, a shred of tobacco stuck on lips to be spit aside. So many careless children without cause for tidy.

Piles of reject clothing were tossed into the main tipi. "No one cares?" I could not fathom such disdain. No rhyme or reason, unless waste and disregard for aesthetics represented the past, a room that had to be cleaned. Embroidering on a jean jacket while the garden went to ruin. Throwing darts to perfect aim while the stove went blank. So, this was joint living! What was my place? My need for order prevailed. I assigned myself meaning by purifying the appropriated, and then defamed, symbol of the tipi. The translucent plastic wrap around its inner circle would regain dignity.

I plucked from the piles discarding poly and selecting intact cotton and wool. I was the commune bag lady! Scraps were useful necessities elsewhere. "Oh, what sign are you? Ah, a Capricorn. That explains it."

Capricorn meant being born under the sign of Saturn, the symbol was the goat with dark influences. Why astrologically, Saturn is considered to be the planet of limitations and hardship, representing tough lessons and our relationship with order, authority, and responsibility was clear to astrologers. To me it resonated with how sullen, dark or judgmental I could be rather than light hearted. How important organization and doing a right thing without waste or ruin was to me. Michael Carpenter interpreted every sign to have its upper and lower dimensions. One could be the lofty mountain goat peering over far dimensions or the lowly barnyard goat tethered to a post and running the rut deeper and deeper.

How petty felt my complaints. Delinquent life was running its course. So much depends on chaos and order. Without having their contrast, the one without the other, we drearily decline.

"And what messy sign are you?

"Our meals were filling and basic. Diners were relieved to be fed. I rarely heard complaints, except from me, about the greasy ring scumming the dish pans left by inept dishwashers with lesser attention to infection. Sounds like I was a mom figure! Well part of me was! I had no idea how to deal with sharing responsibility. And I was a 23-year-old elder. A partial remedy came from Michael and Annie who arrived with a gift of wooden bowls for all.
Someone constructed identifying cubicles on the outside cookshack wall, to scrub or not, one's own bowl. "Who took my bowl?? Damn it!"

Chuck

CL, Chuck, Chas, Chauncey, Charles depending upon his or your relationship. Chuck was testing the deluge of opportunity. He was young when I met him, a mere 19, and had an ornery mean streak about stupidity. He was ironic with caustic humor and astute when listening to meaningful conversation. But his being uninhibited offered the most appeal under a swab of unruly distinguishing hair. As facsimile secretariat of the JP, he took mental notes on the residents, the aspiring movers and groovers, the data seeking sociologists, the naturalists and the voyeurs and could account for accomplishments, donations, and misdeeds. His tallying of visitors led to a count towards 800. That record keeping was most of what we knew of newcomers and individuals, often devoid of last names. He had grown up on Long Island in a situation that did not nurture his individuality. He described how he had taken a tv onto the ridge pole of his Long Island family suburban roof and blasted the neighborhood like a tomcat claiming territory. His parents were confounded but familiar with resistance for Chuck was a Red Diaper Baby, called that as an offspring of parents sympathetic to values of communism. Mike and Muriel returned from a Paul Robeson concert aglow with the force of being in the presence of greatness. Liberalism went only so far, for even when I was pregnant, Muriel refused for us to share the same bedroom. "Not in my house! You're not married." I was familiar with her values and it was their house. I slept in their other son's room with its own tv.

Chuck had enrolled at a now defunct college in VT, Mark Hopkins, where he met Michael, Annie and Fritz. He played hooky at an in-town apartment and flourished with like-minded. They perversely served hors d'œuvrés to an ill-advised instructor, spreading cat food pâté on crackers, ruined weak wooden chairs and enjoyed the life of the newly liberated. The landlord sued them for damages. I donated my VW to defray the fine and received in the stead, their gratitude and inner circle. I did not care much for possessions for I had never truly suffered. My family life had unfurled with protective coating.

I had little inclination to go to Woodstock in Aug 1969, as I knew there would be more of the same, an invasion the caliber and color overdosed at the JP. I yearned instead for quiet nature and solitude. After everyone returned, CL followed me to my tipi. He followed me and we talked all night. An eclipse. I'd assumed he'd disdained me along with almost everyone else in his aloof way. On the surface were words and misleading impressions. I was receptive, fascinated, innocent, unconscious. Dawn showed and he was gone. We had talked all night proving we could. For those of us practicing free love some berated as promiscuity, chastity was an obvious waste of youth and pleasurable opportunity. We would not deny the rebellious touch of our generation. But savoir faire about good timing was attractive and very cool. I found appeal in that he did not ask to or expect to share my sleeping bag. Soon after, we just stayed together.

When I was ready to try love, it came like a solid thunk and landed heaving and breathy, the sure sound of heavy bales thrown from rafters onto planks far below.

Grapes

None of us had superior skills required for creating and managing group order but as romantics we were willing participants. There was no means of oversight nor effective planning and few scant meetings in the less than two years I was there. One organizational meeting focused upon how to pay the taxes and mortgage. Ten of us relocated to Lake Canandaigua to a Carpenter family cabin, to hire out as vineyard workers. We accepted the generosity and idealism of the Carpenter matriarch, Floss. We were good workers manicuring branches and pruning the first grapevines I'd ever seen. We paid our dues.

Chuck fed me hors d'oeuvres, supermarket cheese on wheat crackers with the aplomb and tenderness of the elite, tiny bite size room temperature pieces to savor and kiss. Jeff slept in the loft above our bed. How unnerving to see him peering over the edge down on our love. For us, free love included abandoning inhibitions and for him, he could not help but be a voyeur. Annie exclaimed that she had never seen Chuck "so enamored. He must really like you!" And that is how I felt.

Fritz

Beautiful Fritz. Restless Fritz who loved men. One night years later during his visit to Montague with no spare bed for him, I offered to share my space. "I just don't sleep with women." He was a secure gay guy to have expressed himself so straight. "It's ok Fritz. Just go to sleep. No problem. Can I hug your back?" I call him beautiful because so many of our young people were in early stages of power and freshness and because he was beautiful. His mouth created new shapes as he espoused, criticized or sang. Thick hair fell to one side, expressive of mischief. His prominent ball joints made me stare at his solidly well formed body. He was a cultural ambassador from the communes who elected to foray into the communities beyond our borders to meet the locals, to enhance intellectual hunger in the expansive corridor of new acquaintance.

He had lived in NY State prior to the JP. His father was a judge whose otherworldly advice and attitude Fritz inherited. And so Fritz charmed me. "Which apples would you eat first from the cellar barrel? The best ones or the ones that are starting to go by? Why the best of course." And, "On me it don't stink!" Very different from my old world inheritance, those who fled pogrom and conscription and survived with humble precious commodity.

One day returning from a town trip, we cut through the woods and came upon the country home of the famous pianist Rudolph Serkin. Fritz had been invited company of the family and so felt at liberty to further enjoy with us, the ice cream in their outdoor freezer. What conscious audacity.

One did not know when Fritz would appear, for the privacy of his wanderings protected his emerging identity. In the era when gays were sorely abused, he felt safe in his chosen circles, proud to be gaily himself without having to announce to the world his fantastic revelation. Then when he did appear, he had bright stories about the farming village of Guilford and further on into the political enclaves of Brattleboro. Fritz knew he did not want to settle at the JP but would work somewhere, like the sawmill, until he made enough money to buy his own land where he would work with oxen, have honey bees, a still and a cider press.

Push pull, the moral dilemma. "Push the wrong button; pull the wrong plug,"[12] follow orders, salute, pull the trigger now!

CL and Fritz had time to prepare for their draft board physical on the same date at the same place. They were not conscripts who could or would obey orders. They were do it yourselfers, confident in their ability to convince in interview they were unfit for military duty, not presenting written assurance from a shrink that the subject was unhinged and unfit for duty in some generic way. . And that was true. Do you resist and go to jail [13] or avoid the draft and flee the county? Or "Do I enlist?" the other compelling question some friends chose. The ultimatums were strict and offered no choice for them. Entering the military was a sure as hell NO. They could fell trees for survival but never on command, pull a trigger.

Their commitment was not Biblical but parallel to this:

In Deuteronomy IX-XX, we are directed to prioritize and preserve trees even during time of war, especially food bearing trees, despite the urgency of battle. One of The Ten Commandments ordered, "Thou shall not kill." The Bible did not outlaw slaying in wartime. With or without the Bible, they would not take orders.

Fritz clutched Chuck's side like a mommy figure and theatrically up-played an identifying characterization as weak. CL drank 40 cups of caffeine, stayed up all night, smeared himself with compost. "Get me outta here!" he bombarded the claustrophobic hearing room compartment. They were rejected with a get them out of here confirmation and we were saved that mortality.

---

12   Quote from Green Mt Press film *Save the Planet* a child's response to the nuclear dilemma

13   Dear friend of later days, Randy Kehler had spent two years incarcerated. His resistance to war and his courageous motivation inspired Daniel Ellsberg to release *"The Pentagon Papers."*

Janice

When someone wonderful enters your life, energy is transmitted. Optimism expands possibility. So it was when Blondie appeared. I call Janice that affectionally now, though she may not respond well to implications. But when Janice arrived, I recognized worth beneath her voluptuous wealth of hair for she was a woman with purpose beyond pleasure. Her partner Josh had staked out their haven in escape from the draft. My liking Josh made it likewise easy to accept her. She reckoned how to maneuver in our roughened house and shared in the all-consuming work of making a home and especially a kitchen that functioned, fed many and was relatively clean. Try that with no running water. Large cheap pots easily burned while char filled the impending burn holes. There were few creative cooks among us and fewer willing to confront the erratic stove. Simple ingredients, rice, beans, tahini, peanut butter and onions could be designed in few ways.

Janice invented desserts. Those "dining" were expectant and content. As I could determine, Janice let no one take advantage of her. She was strong willed and could let shrill a ball park whistle from between her fingers that would call all dogs.

Janice had sinuous muscles that moved under her skin as she chopped upon the less than solid chopping block. Kindling was rare. One might have thought with all those people and the forest surround, we'd have surplus! While some of us toiled, motivation was clearly too sophisticated for some who then played cards, crocheted important doodles on their jackets or turned the crank on the record player, a revered actuality.

Janice had foresight without needing direction. She wasted no time. Her fingers were raw from some prior mishap. Still we scrubbed and hauled and became communal kin. She manipulated financing for food and we would slip away to Richard B's cabin where she and Josh would retreat at night. She especially liked gorgonzola cheese and wheat crackers and took care to supply us with extra nutrients for pregnancy.

Josh's Concerns

Josh was a favorite newcomer, a member of a patched rebellious tribe with headband and leather wristband. He was the soon to be father of Janice's unborn, Sequoya. He was a kind natured participant in daily communal functions, had no obvious deficits, and was a Coloradan city guy come to the Baby Farm to escape penalties from draft resistance, booze and urban strife. With evident virtues of observing what needed to be done, his enticing smile charmed. He was a honkytonk spirit, a country blend of slap the knees and clap the hands. He loved his inaccessible wine and called himself a wino trying to straighten out. Josh had not smoked dope for one year, an indication of determination. Wagging his toes, sitting cross legged, he waited to get strung out on buttered popcorn.

Janice recalled the notorious STP clan from Boulder, Colorado. Three escorted Josh to the JP although they departed, disaffected and bored in the woods. Janice had never directly gotten involved with them but she knew Deputy Dawg and recalled that he was camping in the "Nederland" where she met Josh. "They were gross, crazy and abusive and I'm not sure how close Josh was with them." Along with JP laxity, came undesirable proposals. "I see you when you pee out there in the field. I like the way you wipe." Creepy! No shame as if Dawg had been praising millet. Familiar with unwanted approaches, I sucked my teeth and forced retreat. Mostly we were spared from vulgarity.

Smokey

Oh those boys! Smokey sauntered onto the premises and I recognized one of the most casually attractive young men. He did not strut beauty nor await attention like handsome people are used to. He even pretended his attractiveness was nonexistent. His Sagittarian force was exclusive of the bow. He walked high narrow beams or a tight-rope of fallen trees spanning a ravine. A slip was turned into a dance step. He had the onset of a demonstrable trade which few of us had developed. He ingeniously knew about living in the woods, identifying trees, using tools effectively, sharpening blades, starting fires.

Smokey invited me, "Come! Just come!" I followed for if he had something to share on top of the adjoining hill, it would be worthwhile. He hoisted me to climb reachable branches of a great pine tree, an easy enough tree to climb once access was gained. Solid limbs splayed like rungs. Ascending through branches dense with needles, nothing was clearly seen beyond the moment of grasp and rise until the next limb straight up and all was hold on and rise higher. He urged me to the top aerie where he initiated supple winged motion, the magic of a pendulum uside down in reverse and we were the arc, the push and pull where nothing inhibited but the tinges of possibility. Whoosh to and fro. I became double my person in that upper canopy of bird land, super human, unrestrained and mesmerized. Pine tree. The earth offered nothing more grand. We swayed and filled our lungs, air expressive and plump with oxygen and flight. Smokey had bequeathed how to leave myself behind and to know comfort in an altered state, corporeal but not, for we were the end branches of a tree. I immaterialized the problems down below. We could see what birds saw. He swayed us in the canopy back and forth in their world. "No, it won't crack off! I guess!"

Smokey knew good timing, fish and reel. His talent of patience had him recognize and catalogue reclusive caverns that edged under rocks in fishing spots. Later he carved and painted hundreds of fish art and thousands of wooden shingles. Curled red oak and cedar remains were perfect kindling for bushels of gifts.

Smokey had friends at the experimental Franconia College, a going out of business one-time estate, with irregular squeaky floor plateaus and tilted hallways that recur in distracting dreams. The slouching students (what were they studying) appeared stoned or in vogue, appropriately depressed. Our plan was to hitchhike north into Vermont. No one accepted us into their car until a pick up truck pulled over. We would have gotten into any vehicle as the weather was formidably frigid. There was only room on the back platform where we crushed closely, ice bitten digits and frozen rears, a disadvantage to hitchhikers. As reminiscing seniors, those misadventures would be inscribed as floridly absurd adventure.

Smokey chortled about running naked to the wood shed with Red Mitchell, to saw and chop for starting the morning stove, then charging back again to bed. Fond brotherhood of the nightly marble championship, especially with Josh, displayed cat eyed collections. Candle light was often extinguished by wind through trans-continent apertures. Smokey popped the baking banana into his mouth just because we said he could not. He relayed how much alcohol had actually been consumed. There in the wood shed was the double burden of wood and lines of empties. He had lugged drunken Josh in from the frozen skies to bed that night of the fire, a horrid memory which overshadowed memory. Life is so battering.

Chris and John

Chris and John. Chris and John, a loving refrain. I had moved into their tipi but did not meet them until Chuck and Fritz and I drove a delivery car cross country to LA then up the Big Sur coast to Berkeley.

In LA we stayed for a night at a mansion of a JP friend. We were consigned willingly to the pool boy's house. The orange trees were in full production but the mother would only purchase brightly colored plastic wrapped fruit. We understood why her daughter had abandoned such a life, although as far as we were to know, it was temporary.

In Berkeley, we aligned with Chris and John in friends' apartments though they slept in their neatly retrofitted bread truck. It sported wooden shelves, an adequate cooking arrangement, a bed and settee. That vehicular home on wheels performed reliably, for John was one of those build and fix guys, an idea man. He'd enter a room and infuse us with contagious enthusiasm, from the simplest edible, "Here are corn nuts. What? Never heard of them? You're on the West Coast," to "We can make some spare cash by selling "Berkeley Barbs," "Tribes" and "Good Times," local alternative papers. "Let's drive up to Mendocino to Long John's family camp" which used to be a retreat for the rich. Long John had found us at the JP in his de-escalation from upper crust. He was a generous curious soul, neither aware nor inquisitive about making the basics of communal life easier. Visiting him in his out back was gratifying payback and he welcomed us at his rustic though degenerated multi cabined redwood inheritance.

Chris and John were positive models. In their cabin, the cook stove was boiling a giant pot of dog food: home ground grain plus butcher shop bones and suet, the survivalist's do it yourself save money method.

Chris was the funniest casual ragamuffin by choice. If she were dressed in lace, she'd look like a Renaissance lady, hair controlled of course, another beauty whose upper lip was shaped expressively wide and whose profile stunned

Grecian art history. See her schlepping through the mud, her raggedy pants legs longer than her legs and always that navy pea coat. She was boldly straightforward. We knew her opinion when it counted. "That asshole's not coming to live with us. I don't even like him. He uses people. He's not even able to love them first."

Chris was reinventing herself after too much actual dropping out and a chaotic family life. Her mother was an internationally acclaimed surgeon who operated on disfigurements in children elsewhere. Her own five or six children took relative care of themselves along with the storied step-father and two brothers with fatal genetic disease. Chris was in a mode of personal rehab. Her acute dry wit and curiosity, her macro south western cooking, and willingness to share her space, made her receptive and alluring material for enduring friendship. Later when my life took precarious turns, I would relocate to their home where they offered comfort and temporary retreat.

Chris and John eventually became founders of Martha Vineyard's South Mountain Co, a cooperatively owned, run and worked construction company that inventively used salvaged material from flooded areas and rejection "debris" from demolition. And they co-invented co-housing projects on the island and elsewhere. John's book *The Company We Keep* [1] tells the story well.

---

1   *The Company We Keep* Chelsea Greene Pub 2008

More Fritz

Years later at the annual May Day celebration at Packer Corners, PC, Fritz came close with something to reveal. He was HIV positive. The disease had caught him in the common grip of reckless sex. For him, sex was not uncomplicated as it was for most heterosexuals, most of whose sexually transmitted diseases could be cured with antibiotics. But for him, in the early era of scant misleading HIV information and treatment, sex proved fatal. He explained himself something like this. "I was wild in Brazil. Fucking men was acceptable and common. I had no limits for the first time in my life. I guess I went too far!"

We were so hopeful. What have you tried? How about a strict brown rice diet? Chris Abrams and I usually suggested macrobiotic ph balance for disease. He chortled and carried on with humble bravado and skepticism. Decades later, Chris and I talked about how she had tried that remedy for her relentless brain cancer. The last time I saw Fritz he had succumbed to and lost himself to AIDS. "Quit looking at me!" How ravaging gross humiliation can be. He and his darling Tony (not Mathews) enjoyed part nership. Tony soothed me. "He says that to everyone." Fritz is one of many of our commune family now dead. My list obviously expands as we age.

Grandpa Rosner would say about loss, "Such is life." I agree, minus the flattening of philosophical tautology.[2] "Boys will be boys!" What? Does this deferentially excuse bad behavior? Reminiscent echoing has Grandpa Rosner's voice in my ear, to revisit how stalwartly Morris and Rebecca dealt with what could have been abysmal loss of country, child, livelihood and savings. If stoicism avoids submission, then I receive that family trait well. "It is what it is!"

---

2   Tautology is philosophically redundant refrain without deeper meaning which thereby precludes a retort.

Judie

Judie had a pet raccoon, Perdikee. She was the in-house animal aficionado assuring that any animal was given fair treatment and food. She loved to bake a smoky kitchen version of brownies. What a hoot with her outbursts of laughter and reminiscences of a crazy private school with head master who loved young girls. When she returned intermittently to the city, she stayed with a woman who housed several chimpanzees in her pungent Village apartment. Judie was truly a pet person. The JP had no restrictions about animals and so the inmates wandering the country brought dogs, too many of which would come charging the front door from the hill at first signs of breakfast. It was a voracious descending onslaught. Judie was kind to them all.

Red Mitchell and Dennis

Two buddies showed up and were especially appreciated for charm, music, participation and strength. Mitchell moved to Martha's Vineyard and married into island gentry with acreage, a sheep farm, and a farmer's acumen about how to create fertile soil in places like well grazed pasture land. Dennis moved to rural Northern California and supported agriculture. Both have maintained close ties with Chris and John.

Parties

Despite serious flaws, there was also exultation. Meals and gifts appeared from outsiders. Parties sprung at Packer Corners, PC, the commune farm nearer the other entry of our dirt road. Picture the JP motley crew trudging the spring ruts for the short enough mile, pregnant Janice's and my creation, a wok of fried rice and vegetables, displayed proudly by the carriers. Other sister farms were Montague and Wendell. We were connected by college, politics, agriculture, art, intimacies, drugs and music. May Day, an international celebration of worker's struggles, was our celebration. In gay revelry we viewed ourselves as workers too, or we admired the spirit. Home movies exist of Stevie stirring a huge concoction over the fire. Perhaps someone donated rare seafood tidbits to enhance the potion. Dinner and dancing.

"I can hardly see your face."
"Cold out here, even in May."
"Put another log on!"
"It's over by the garage apartments."
"Beware the ruts!"
"Beware the sink holes!"
"A bit damp!"
"Throw it on. It'll burn. Eventually!"
"Ahhh!"

Our rock and roll band rumbled the hills. Then came the bongo bongers who without pause, satisfied by rhythm, to loosen and free and connect with primitive.

Richard, exultantly, was the sprightly satyr dancing on toes like a mythological goat herder. Pound the dirt, turn and express what-you-will, pass "le jwan" but be wary of who put what in the punch.

"It's not spiked. That got drunk before you got here."

Fritz, our Mick Jagger Bad Boy sang in "Sympathy for the Devil" with glistening lips close to the mic. Chuck wore his American Flag "overhauls" in proud display. We walked to the pond where we plunged. Our hair, long, uncouth, the thick part was congealed at the nape. Beautiful young bodies tested the icy water, our granules, grounded and smoothed on that rainy day.

"Ohhhh, you have a hard on. Get it in the water. Even with ice, you've got the most amazing thing."

"What are you guys talking about?"

"Oh, something!"

Breaking Down

Outside the common house, two uncompromising men wrestled in the snow. They showed teeth and twisted figures. I was absorbed, not frightened. Brawling, angry and nude, how perfect bare skin, ever tightened from the icy surface, masculine and dominant. It was dereliction of the hippie soul. Foolish deep unexplained anger expressed as valor, defending communal ethics. What was it over? A pillow, Gypsy said, but I knew better. "I can't stand that selfish punk!" My god! The theater, a divine comedy while wrestling the snow. Later, I put cold compresses on bruises and bruised spirit.

Manly means something. Manly means... well it could mean... but then again it also means... it means...

How about self-confident and kind?

But why did he combat the log?

He just felt like wrestling the log! That's why!

Why don't you cut it in half, save some time?

A new comer's rough authoritarian female voice broke in, "Come on fellas. Break it up." "Sandy, Sandy, Sandy." And "What do you do with the dogs? Just leave them out there? Oh well another Dog Thing." And Leslie, poor girl, had an impossible crush on Fritz. She usually floated around with her balalaika, a triangular mandolin type guitar. I noticed that no one seemed to recognize how earnestly she strummed. I continued to see potential in the commune livers. An aspiring artist, a musician, a therapist, a linguist. No matter that I shrugged and rolled my eyes at the wasteland. I maintained delicate hope that enough curious and thoughtful activists would join us and mend the fray, but then they too were passing through.

Fritz was a dominant Leo, so Michael, a balancing act Aquarian, would just be Michael and meet on a friendly level of acceptance. He'd throw in his own wisdom while smiling gently, shrewdly. Annie would naturally see some bullshit to specify while uninhibitedly exposing a dripping breast, nursing, nursing, nursing that precious well fed babe. Hippie mothers publicly wore nursing babies like banners of liberation from hide-your-breast inhibitions. Michael said something discordant and despite feeling clumsy to challenge him, I rebelled against his accept everyone philosophy. He did not retort but offered scant inanity like "We are all one." Tut tut tut ad nauseum around the circle. I turned to the Bugler and rolled a cigarette. Someone provided one five pound can of something that smelled oppressively like Gauloises, that acrid, pungent, stinky French let's be cool brand.

A lone figure, not a hippie, caught my interest because of his slow pace, erratic and yet rhythmical while he hummed, "Bum, bum, ba da da da da" as if in an operatic trance. He raised a closed umbrella over his whitewall haircut, a long beige belt hung below his raincoat. There was Long John and Little John even though he was not so little. Baby John and Bubba and of course Louisiana Long John. And David Starfish with pop out black curls, whose clear sockets were filled with almost innocent honesty. His jester costumes were distracting. But his yes smile endeared.

The Bus People arrived, maneuvering their habitable bus into a space from which it may never have been extricated. One guy, two wives, not too much obvious jealousy, a baby and what a happy family. Love, love, love those sycophants. His people called him Doctor No, I did not know why, and they sat at his feet as he corrected them with ditties, adapted Lao Tzu prophesies about love, simplicity and patience. Had he engaged the fundamental quote, "Those who govern people make them discontented with being controlled and therefore cause them to be uncontrollable." But not so! He was met with stunned, adoring how-wise-you-are-eyes. Nancy laid out the Tarot and with moist lips, read spidery eyed interpretations. Bob, a make shift Jesus look alike, entered naked under his robe, threw out directives like tut and bathing suit, tut, tut and modesty, au natural. Turn the other cheek; everyone is a brother. Would he share his lush robe? Nancy said Bob loved everyone first. Too many apostles were draining the pot. Loving everyone took what I was unwilling to donate. Was this to be a commune in name only?

Noel's stocking feet entered the room. He just stood there. It seemed like he was wondering what he should do next. "If blah blah like I said last night, then blah blah blah. But where can I go? There's even dog food here and I wonder what will be for breakfast. They brought me here. Maybe I'll push on. Gosh, I wonder if they like me... Oh well..."

Desi was a mix of toy land and childhood Catholic austerity. Another was adolescent, nearly virginal and yet had suggestive eyebrows. That one would soon start sitting cross legged and point a finger at who would talk next. A famous ego lounged over there.

Without deft inquiry about age, ancestry or origins, we were occupied with our own identities, food, too many dogs, wood or the weather. There were abundant unacceptables. The guests brought guests. Easy by comparison was the un-fluctuating snoring that turned into the rev of a motorcycle. But sickly arrogant Macro John askew with theories strained my limits. I wanted to concentrate and it was obvious some-one wanted to interrupt. Carole revealed an infection on her leg she had kept hidden for some time. We provided antisep-tic ointment and bandages. Stupid girl washed herself in the community pot. She needed her own commune. No sooner did we start to get to know the collection of us as a whole, then there was departure, days passed and new strangers ar-rived. We worked together and slowly strangeness departed. Two were like little kids, staying late in bed, playing checkers, reading Dr. Zeus stories, meshing privately but nothing more creative. A body stooped to stoke the fire. The hordes carried ideals in their shoulder packs. I was curious about possibility and layers of personality beyond initial impressions so I tried to receive newcomers as the JP was devised.

Chuck noted that so and so seemed less haughty that day.

"He's very proud," I said.

"Haughtiness isn't a particularly positive quality."

"If so and so had called for help, would he have been haughty or meek?"

Judy and I escorted each other, not to the defunct slit trench, but to the newly constructed outhouse, not A+ solid, but one step up. She would not enter the unpredictable sturdiness of the shack. Being a discerning person, she much preferred to squat even on toilets then to settle above an unexamined spidery cavity. We squatted in the snow. It was below freezing for winter had arrived with sleet then freeze then sun then freeze again. There came riveting crisp cracks resounding from footsteps as if the pasture were opening to gulp us down, ground thunder of cracking thin ice over a wide expanse. We had restrained so long, our pee made sharp holes and fat lines. We wiped with snow. Then the sick girl who cried a lot came bolting to the outhouse, her first appearance on account of she had not eaten in three days. "You know you can go to the hospital." She defended her withdrawal with, "That's square. Not natural." Yet she rummaged through the tub of pills searching in the candle light for something to pop. The stupidity of it all bonded Judy and me.

Samples of overheard comments

Amelia Earhart was rumored to be alive at 73 in New Jersey.
The last time they went to the moon it rained for two weeks.
De Gaulle is dead. Nothing special. Who cares?
Full Taurus moon on Friday the 13th.

In contrast to the air of absurd, was the air of revolution. Will it come, an apocalypse like Yeats' spirit of the world in his poem *The Second Coming*?

> ...Turning and turning in the widening gyre
> The falcon cannot hear the falconer;
> Things fall apart; the center cannot hold;
> Mere anarchy is loosed upon the world...

We could feel the gyre, spinning faster until all hell would break loose and spit us out. European countries were paving over historical cobblestone streets so the cobbles could not be used as ammunition. A working payphone in the big city could not be found.

We fathomed Bob Dylan's messages as in his song "The Times They Are a Changin'".[14]

What I mulled was what the country would become, for look who was here to run or inherit it. "We dance round in a ring and suppose. But the secret sits in the middle and knows."[15]

Chuck returned from visiting friends at PC feeling dispirited to integrate with uninspiring strangers at his home. He may not have felt like he was part of a family, but he was integral. Desi came breathless, "Chuck, come help Andy. Come! I don't know exactly but he may have broken something." Chuck, the unofficial data keeper of the comings and goings of "riff and raff" in trivial pursuit, was not absolved from the impact of so many newcomers. His sympathies flourished with the intellectual and political exchange at PC.

Walk to the door. Feel the gravel beneath bare feet. She sits there wiping her nose on a green towel. Touch your finger to, to, to, not to her forehead, but to your button to see if it is right. "Hey she cried, come back. Kiss me goodbye." Onto the porch, crowded and crouching, she protected her wounds.

What was there to do? We kept on changing and did not agree with opinions of even a day before. An announcer on radio said, "The government should definitely subsidize these teenagers, especially the girls!"

There were furtive glances towards the small mirror, a faded one at that, balanced on a two by four ledge. It was one minor vice we might enjoy but accepted that it was not cool to check one's image often, a lingering insecurity or vanity. Other anxieties might be appeased by brushing the hair, caring enough to work out the snags, eating brown sugar out of the box, having sex again and again, pretending to belong to someone or someplace or reading and reading, reading and reading.

We were depleted with too much sharing. Yet JP was

---

14   "...There's a <u>battle</u> outside ragin'...For the <u>times</u> they are a-changin'"Bob Dylan

15   Robert Frost poem

home. Chuck's sweeping was upsetting a lot of dust. I opened the window and was bathed by the Beatles' lyrics, "Here comes the sun. It's all right."

And so we made a baby. We were after all, on the Baby Farm and that is what love produced.

Egg and sperm infinitum and then recognizable fetus, armed with sounding demands of "Me first!" that cracked like a beloved wailing whip and the tender unprepared spigot where milk flowed in stimulus to any baby's cry, even in a movie theater. Milk spouted like a fountain from the taut repository with no pantry for excess.

"I always thought you were big breasted but I suppose I only saw you when you were pregnant or nursing!" said one male friend.

Ah, those breast men. And this is my ode to the economics of E F Schumacher's "Small is Beautiful."

The Green River
and Neptune

If you can picture this, you will understand something about our identity. A steamy assortment of us from our ti-pis and tents, had gone to meet our newfound neighbors at a swimming hole, the greenless Green River. The river was gushing with rain and currents, cold in contrast to the swel-tering day. We caroused publicly for this was a free flowing river. A varied lot we were, whose wild apparitions gripped and stunned judgmental faces into dubious rejection. The uninhibited nature of our hippie frolic, robbed the monopoly held by notorious Haight Ashbury.

Bathing in the river was delight and necessity. What did people really smell like if they ate differently, were junk food-ies, macro-biotic or vegetarian? We ascribed to the Beatles message, "You are what you eat." We had ostensibly rejected advertising hype, deodorants, so called beauty enhancing balms. Different smells were detectable, some pheromones more irresistible but all smelled good after the purifying dunk.

The men were half bare in jean cut-offs, unusual swim suits compared to trunks of the locals. Hair was corded back with leather thongs salvaged from work boots or let to flow comfortably free like women. The women wore underwear as fancy as the Riviera or in liberally flowing dresses. Anything to keep us from the law and close to water revival.

Village teens gaped advantageously from boulders infat-uated by cliché interpretations of sex, drugs and rock and roll of "Those hippies!" not much older than themselves nor much different except in shag and hair. Our group was not overtly sexual but scandal could not help but identify us. Not much existed beyond the pleasure of the moment. Were the locals freaked? Was the body too exposed beneath the makeshift bathing suit? We did not care. We were unfazed by observation. As we descended the embankment, we at least didn't shed our clothes.

Neptune, a Puerto Rican refugee from the city, was climbing to the top of the covered bridge to swan dive. All eyes were on his spider climb as he gained the open face of the roof. "Hey, you can't be up there!" reprimanded one outraged censor, a self-proclaimed authority figure. Neptune was not deterred He dove to test the spring. True to his name, he plunged like an Olympic porpoise down, down and swoop curved up to avoid boulders and survive the shallows below. He and comrades were visiting to check out the scene, scope the possibilities for escape from gang vendetta, temporarily abandoning their posts and retreating to the extraordinarily open commune for cooling off. We were receptive. No questions had to be answered; no one thought it mattered. If ours was a place of sanctuary, the Ricans were alluring, rare in that place and welcome. Until the proprietor of the country store wary of the foreigners, complained about shoplifting. We had a sensitive meeting to address differing values and reputation.

Calamitously, Neptune and cohorts did eventually return to city knives and gang warfare which did a ruinous job. The city required their blood. Acid was thrown in one's face, splotching the winning skin to raw pink and emptying an eye socket.

Our friends appeared on the steep bank consuming the incline in a bedlam of vision. I recall three. The queen was flanked by her kings. She led the way with grace in a black leotard which thinly covered the fluidity of her flesh. Hey, pretty close to a bathing suit! Her spicy mouth was hallooing to us and exclaiming in descent and especially in the touch and entry to the cold river. The men, coy by comparison, picked their way down the gravel incline, exclaiming gaily with smiles of approval and counter-approval of life, of each other and this particular life sustaining enterprise. Their clothing was peeled to faded swimwear, their laughter contagious while the locals yanked their curious kids away from the danger of us and the surfacing invitation we seemed to suggest, a connection to family gang.

Huck and Susie

   Huck and Susie had been friends who turned out not to be friends. They were a favored couple due to the soulful intensity of his blues harp that excited the air. Susie's spirited laugh matched her untamed orange bush of hair. They were two of the hundreds at our open door who impressed, for they brought music and laughs about rural isolation and the subsequent inaccessibility to get high. Drugs not being allowed was a logical survivalist dictum and kept the police at bay. Huck and Susie had been speed freaks but I did not care much about their pasts, appreciating instead the present tense and helpful hands.

   After a few months, they revealed disreputable ways. I pinpointed empty jars of missing fruit askew by their bed, fruit so laboriously canned almost impossibly by us novices over an open fire pit. Egad! Like sneaky dogs or distractible unmindful kids, they left easy evidence while shoveling the fruit of our labor into their mouths. What assholes with lame excuses like needing an immediate vitamin boost.

   The final resting place for my affections happened in The East Village.

   "Come with us," they offered. "We'll have such a good time. We know the Village and will show you. We have cash." An adventure after months in the country! I was lured.

   We settled in someone's car and were dropped in the W Village amid the throng of street life. Where was everyone going? Thousands of hippies, their bright clothes living in lofts, the free free life which seemed as simple as supplying food, sofa or score, or as uncomplicated as painting a canvas all one color and having it appear as different as opposites. So many people roaming. So many attitudes of cool and rebellion. No suits, no church purses but bare city feet or sandals and flowing garb.

   Huck and Susie needed to separate to find a friend. Their plan to meet at six turned to nine. Where were they? I had joined this trip because they offered to show me the ropes. I became one of the wanderers, hoping to spot them on the packed streets.

   Neptune miraculously appeared and was pleasantly startled to see me. He knew they were on the other side of town, the E Village. Strikingly gracious, he became a willing guide with no covert motives. I, a country mouse with ill fitted shoes for a cross town hunt, followed down barely lit though safer streets, his milieu. He knocked familiarly on doors, gallant even in urine soaked halls, passing deadbeats with as much focus as if they were bushes. Then we came to the young girl's place, she who looked old beyond her years, her airy knee out perpendicular to the floor, foot propped on the chair searching for the vein to pop. The girl's eyes were blackened rubber and cheated of youth. She plunged into a thigh with no skin to spare.

I had witnessed the power of heroin before, not in passing a sprawled addict, but when a friend woke me with the urgency of death, "Walk me, walk me or I'll die."

Neptune backed us out and continued to lead, inspecting buildings, searching, searching, and eventually he opened the correct door to find lion and lady both in the guise of Huck and Susie. Huck was mechanically brushing at his fuzzy out hair as if anything could smooth his brain. His wild expression was one of indulgence and narcissism. TRIP! Susie held an extravagant smile and avowed that they had just been coming to get me. They were high. But not hippie high. Addict high! And that made me, to both of my erstwhile "friends," a nobody.

From an advantage of straight normalcy, I derived release from their hold. Since they had no personal gear, I took note not to trust contact, a verified way to catch something legged in those vagabond times.

They were evicted from my inviolate inner ear. I was not Puritan but deceit and abandonment were final dishonors. It was not easy to have it revealed who people could be. We lived in idealistic cloudy time while trying to invent community.

A Loose Bull

A pack of coyotes howl. They tilt their throats to the sky. The air vibrates their concussion. The alfa male howls loudest and long. His pack yip yip yips. Eerie coyote howls claim and chill. What are they howling about? Territory? The dog across the brook? They howl because they are coyotes?

A loose bull will charge the china shop. In an insistent rush, a bull after heat bulldozes barbed wire. A runaway train jumps the track and according to physics, loses itself as a vehicle of comfort and transport.

In the pathos of decline, unpredicted, yet predictable, precautions are nonsensical. Put on your raincoat, it might rain while the bombs are dropping. If you don't know what could happen, then you don't know about unleashed anarchy. Only a few rules separated us from undoing on that night-of-no-censorship. There were those who dismissed the rules, glibly flaunted their indiscretions. No finger pointing enforcer curbed us. This was a living experiment of freedom and equality. There was disparity of age, degree of commitment, maturity and obscure desperation.

Someone dominates the unattractively christened "shithouse." Someone howls and howls. "Aooooooo. Aooooo." Who is it?" Gypsy responds in kind. His gleeful, somewhat demented elated shimmer chafes while his yearning soul drifts and waits a turn. A single incident says so much about our shedding restraints, as if a howl brings one closer to the wild. Smokey said he's seen a strange hulking shape the last two nights on the edge of the real wild.

Dizzy Desiree had another tantrum. She said she left the commune to see if she'd miss it. Then she called it "Home." Does typical youth, absorbed with pressing self-absorbed matters of identity, comprehend others? We recognized character by what was given and taken. But I had no idea how many people I even lived with! Chuck said he loved my almost everything but that I complained a lot. Well things were not good enough. Differences loomed in that I thought I wanted to be part of the people and he was apart. Pregnant Carol, Scott, Patty, Janice, Smokey, Gypsy, Leslie, Jeff, Shawn, Roughage, Joshua, Adam, Jeremy, Betty Boop, Fritz, The Carpenters, here one day, gone too soon...

Politics and the power of hormones fulfilled our consciousness as did harsh truths about too many premature deaths: Marshall Bloom from the Montague Farm, Larry in Philadelphia and Joshua Jebb from Rock Bottom. So many people "come and go, talking of..."[16] brown rice! Or millet! Leftovers! Leftover lentils reinvented in a mix with brown rice AND refried.

---

16   T. S. Eliot "The Love Song of J. Alfred Prufrock"

Fire and Ice
Robert Frost 1874-1963

Some say the world will end in fire,
Some say in ice.
From what I've tasted of desire
I hold with those who favor fire.
But if it had to perish twice,
I think I know enough of hate
To know that for destruction ice
Is also great
And would suffice.

Our fire story was this.

Chuck erected a room, an eight by ten built on the flat
bed of an immobile truck abandoned when it had ceased
to crank. It settled on cinder blocks near the rough long
house. Two of us played night time house there and privately staged our relationship away from the horde. We
were free to remember our dreams and to reflect on sui-
cidal moths that dive bombed the candle flame. How little
moths, liberated in darkness, learn about death by fire.

Our room was cushioned by a mattress fitting a knee
high platform, under which were stored two crates of clothing and a carton of sewing material. On a shelf above the
pillows were candles, books, writing paraphernalia, a knife,
toiletries, the fewest implements which made life manage-
able. The space was cozy, colorful, candlelit and heated by
a valued kerosene heater accessible to a morning match.
This smelly source warmed a metal bowl of water for winter libations, an act which also separated us psychically
from animals. A curious jar held a collection of our hair
trimmings, golden hair so unlike any other hair especially in the sun, so golden. We imagined stuffing a pillow of
partnership. Symbolic or actual, the concept enhanced our
joy of union.

Fritz, Chuck and I were adopted as authority figures
because we had education or presented that way. And
we had each other. Unintentionally, attitudes of official
seniority were assumed. We were unlikely veterans not

having experienced many paces, though we had survived hundreds passing through our lives, to view, screw, interview, photograph, suck up on hippie hospitality, or move in. Chuck's mocking sneer secured the rejection of some miscreants and ne'er-do-wells blundering onto "our" communal sod.

We three would sprawl easily, inconsequentially touching and casual in developing intimacy. Between the two men, I observed simpatico of male love without the identity crises of coupling. Having just read Sartre's *No Exit*, I saw myself on the other side of the wall of eternity as the two men enjoyed easy rapport and seemed to prefer each other's conversation. A small pain scaled my consciousness for despite our physical affair, if hypothetically, Chuck had to choose someone for all eternity, I sensed it would be Fritz. Sartre transliterated into my life. I could read the handwriting but followed the sacrificial lamb.

The JP became notorious as a ruined experiment despite anyone's enacted values, creative courage or friendships. The fire need not have been inevitable! The rules and warnings, minimally self-protective caveats, were proclaimed sloppily on the side of the cook shack, omniscient forebodings, the list of no's in lower case so as not to be overly officious. To trespass these statutes would assuredly signal the authorities.

One night, Smokey, Chuck and I were delightedly breaking a rule, four piddling but flagrantly taboo tablespoons of whisky scored from a worker at a dairy farm, a minor misdemeanor we chortled, when viewing the larger picture. We lounged privately in restrained yet comfortable space.

A knock dislodged our stately empire. "What? Come in!" The door opened and I was certain I viewed the nature of a devil. His hair and pointed beard were darkly roasted red. Auburn streaks flickered in the candle light until the wind was excluded, then he rose the few stairs into our quarters. He appeared in stature a half body, a half-man, revealed from the waist up, as if he stood full height, for he was kneeling on the narrow foot of floor available.

We questioned his interruption. A negative impression was augmented further by speckles and craters where hands should have been. I was convinced that here before us in days of enchantment, stood a symbol. I had no compunctions about wearing black. In days of rebellion, black had been the Bohemian badge, brooding, poetic, anarchic, closer to racial harmony than rainbow coalitions. It reflected a Saturnian tilt close to my spirit. On him, darkness expressed a void. His black leather perforated archery gloves, revealed contrasting splotches of skin where hands should have been.

His comportment was resentful despite his request. "Hey! I was told to check in here," he declared carelessly as if we were the office. Fritz was in town, where idealism and frustration of baby farming was left behind to seek conviviality or unsatisfied delights.

In the main house, young newcomers had been directors enough to decide who could grant nightly asylum. "Always room at the inn," according to high spiritual standards. "Stay tonight and we'll see about tomorrow!" He was dismissed with a backward wave. Darkness unbroken by electricity, directed him to the hopeful kids inside. He chauffeured a quick trip to the package store. We'll see about tomorrow. See about tomorrow. See tomorrow. See see see see tomorrow.

An ensuing drunken stupor led to the fire. Candle. Open flame. Unguarded hungry flame. Hip EEEEEE, so young. Pass the jug, swig and chug, swig and chug

"I WON'T CONFORM."

As it was a time of anarchy and change, no one was truly to blame and no one was looking for blame. No single person had rolled onto the candle; we all had. Each floundered in quag and mire while "sane and normal" relatives led lives way back home.

"Stupid!" they had called us.

"Boring, compromising, stuck, square!" we'd reciprocate.

Not all unchartered experience ends in disaster.

Hippies were so young and vital and courageous.

Experimentation and lack of guidance led to destructive avenues, boulevards, superhighways. Is the option to conform? True hippies, no matter how we appeared on the outside even in later life, sustained a philosophical pledge against compromise. We trusted our instincts.

Smokey, Chuck and I heard that roaring incongruous noise in the customary silence of our non-electric atmosphere and because it was so out of place it creeped into us. Throwing open the truck house door revealed the blast of titanic fire devouring the night, broiling roiling heat and blinding color leaping skyward from windows and so soon the roof. Screams and screams, twisted faces and panic pounding the arteries. Bursting! Kindling rafters and combustible skin. Ravenous contour of flame. Devastation was fast.

Smokey and Chuck ran in to save; hair and lashes frizzled. The stairs to the loft crashed down and forced retreat. Attic dwellers leapt from the window, dislodging hip bones in exchange for back wrenching safety, far superior to the crisped bodies deadened behind. Pure mayhem in the thick silence of country.

Somehow, a small town tanker maneuvered the road and sucked from the meager brook, too late, too hot, too huge. Townspeople clustered whispering in muffled horror, the up close presence of neighbors, just people after all. We were in fact, babes in the tell-tale night.

The dark man was never seen again.

The Morning After

The fire was not the first of its kind. Just for us! The heart! The heart! Look into eyes. What do we see?

We waited for dawn and for the nightmare to end so we could awaken and struggle with life. We waited for The Law to wield a mighty hand. But no one came and no law showed and it was day break and clean up time after the terrible flame. A huge stinking wreck.

I was good at clean-up. The first time I met Michael, he chortled ironically (as astrology types tend to do) and sighed with relief, when he heard I was a Capricorn, a stereotypically organized sport who could perhaps bring some order to the chaos. But all the order of human touch was feeble compared to the certain forces of us in that place. The fire was symbolic of that chaos and the anarchy of youths banded loosely under a common roof, and ferocious, it claimed.

Our world was shattered, imploded. Dawn, familiar and assertive, crept in despite objections to face ourselves. Early dawn is colorless; then colors emerge. There lies distinction between knowing and accepting reality. The horizon resumes its place without continuity.

Four perished in the Johnson Pastures fire. Josh, Peter, Mitch and "Regina," four souls memorialized in scant phrases, fire logs, family Bibles perhaps and here. Josh's death was close to our hearts and hard to accept for we had known and related to him more. He was the well loved father of the unborn, disappeared by fire, dispersed by water, not dust to dust but into compact clumps.

Peter and Mitch, from Rochester, the Carpenter's hometown, had been allowed to relocate to the open-armed commune by despairing parents, rather than staying home where the two boys chose truancy over crushing standards of high school. The two teens were offered a reprieve from suspension and were allowed to learn life skills at the off-the-grid commune for a spell. Communal alternative education had seemed   temporarily preferable. Oh boys! You were barely here for a week!

I later became a teacher of complicated high school dropouts like you. Your enthusiasm to greet the day at your own will was boundless. No one to compel or clock you. Mitch did not try to talk much to us elders. He was just glad to be in the country. Peter's smile still flashes and both had willing hands. Beautiful boys.

And "Regina" was how she introduced herself. Succinct verbal credentials. We never knew her real name or situation and it had not mattered until then. Her face had glowed with escape from where she had been and what she hoped to feel. She was in a place that felt safe like what home should have offered. Regina remained a bare identity until revealed by the coroner. A fourteen year old runaway! A darling girl. Big dark curly hair. All of us a modicum of equals, but she bonded with the boys and they cared for each other.

What secrets caused you to flee your home?

How you spread in wingless flight, so free, so free to die!

The coroners arrived at dawn with zippered pouches to relocate un-marrowed big bones, femur and pelvis, blatant indications that four had not escaped, had caught a candle and gone not to sleep but to death. Anyone who has been to a lethal fire can still see flames, the shaking of heads, as dawn illuminates ruin and smolder. A stern fire marshal poked remains. Horrible sounds of bustle relocated another body into the censure of a body bag. And they left with the evidence as if the four had never been and no one from the town came for they knew not what to do.

What did my rake uncover, something to save, to use, to remember? An un-melted steel wok, a recognizable blob of glass, once marbles. The previous gorgeous swirls and cat's eyes now smeltered into an unidentifiable sooty mass, rank emotions of chaos. The shooter was wild. Off the mark! Were we the New Age Crazies, losing our own marbles? Hold on! Hold on! Not dead! Not all of us. Not yet! Not dead! Sure-fire off kilter crazy. Whose turn was next?

Listen! What is that gripping noise? A primal scream-er down at the stream. Hear it in the agony of defeat, down at our water source, the source of cleansing, the symbol of change, where water continues to flow clear. Wailing is different from howling. Wailing has consciousness; to wail is to feel out loud. It is personal. To howl is animalistic; it is a wounded protest. I hear the wailing. He was alone with himself down by the stream. The primacy of defeat resounded in the ruined valley. He responded to horror loudly, the young man I thought I knew the best, yet knew so consequentially little. The fire robbed us of youth. But sanity? Where was that to be found? By determination. But to rebuild what, I did not yet know?

Delicate sifting revealed a few insignificant bones the coroner's care had undignified as part of an incinerated body. I became acquainted with the burbled char of bones, trivial as marble size. I knew immediately what, although not who they were. "We prepared a boney shrine and plant-ed Michael's offering of comfrey where the four corners of the long house had been. It was a private burial for our dead. Oh God, what we went through to grow up. What was this preferable to?

Look, look, what do you see? Who are we now?

That one a gone goner. This one, a ghost. Judie in pain, her bones pushed upwards from the escape leap.

I enveloped Janice, the gestating mother, whose eyes had gone blank. Shock had her numb and stumbling. Tak-ing her on as my own, gave me meaning too, forcing her to eat and tend herself, the next elbow at the table.

Starting with daily needs, I made food on an open fire, scraping for kindling and oatmeal until donations arrived.

We could not lie to ourselves for evidence was blatant. We could not posture innocently. Instead we grappled with how to proceed, how to gaze into each other's eyes. There remained the reality of who was left standing and who one cared to be near. I rejected as companions those whose talk was inspired by superstitions of Southern Vermont, of a lone Black family, Lucy Terry and Abijah Prince, who were tormented by the citizenry and so cast a parting curse on Guilford, the site of destruction being our own valley. Traumatized believers sought exemption from the cause of fire. Some were prone to mythology and fabricated historical half truths. We allowed ourselves to picture being in the presence of others. We wandered the hills feeling Lucy's breath, catching Abijah peering from his ebony shadows, our footsteps synchronizing with theirs. Then purposely, we burst the image and were alone to satisfy less eerie impressions. Our Utopian opportunity! What sophistry was this? Testing, unsure of human nature, even unsure of our own selves. Theoretically alone and knowing not how to guide even ourselves. Trip, stumble and fall. Get up! Change direction. Don't submit. Try again.

Forty years later, I encountered a fireman who'd been at our conflagration. Memory still twisted his mouth as to the hopelessness of battle. I reached out tenderly to thank him and touched his emotional chest. He observed me with wonder, an older stranger in whom he recognized something.

Restorative Power

The restorative power of nature embraces something that need not be foreign in us. We enter the forest injured and distracted and return later, more soothed and calmer. Nature births a commitment in us to live compatibly with nature. Then, what's really hard is to learn how to succeed at that responsibility. We reject, even deny being denigrated or influenced by excess commodity and greed. Yet humans continue striving to possess more and even more.

If we are thoughtful, tick tock, the influence of nature is grand enough to rekindle latent instincts. Nature eases us into original skin.

Do we not strive for freedom all the while knowing we are not fully free?

Who has not yearned?
Is what is yearned for identifiable?

Who has not stood naked in front of the body that is you?

When you stare at your eyes, who do you see?
Is that the person you project to the world?

When have you wanted more?
When have you not wanted more?

TO MONTAGUE via CANADA

Four of us chose to relocate north. Theoretically, there was land to be inhabited and freedom from the draft. We would pioneer the forest and define ourselves on foreign terrain, a major step towards liberation. Being identified as American had become an offensive privilege, an "Ugly American" cliché, a misdirected branding of superiority, and for us, a proclamation of reciprocal rejection.

Chuck and Smokey drove north to Nova Scotia and stumbled upon Alan (sp) Black's family as they picked wild berries off the roadside. Alan invited them to his house to negotiate a land deal in his curiously helpful and secretive manner. The Canadian, cloaked in obscurity, intimated past ties with arcane presidential secret service deals. Was he furtive and paranoid or a personality dictated to by austerity of long winters and scrabbling?

Alan directed the men to a recommended fishing hole. He would collect them down river at dusk. That unanticipated two sided coin was where trout abounded along with heinous mosquito attack as the sun descended. The fishermen raced to where Alan waited. He roared at their innocence and their adversaries. We purchased 160 acres of uncharted forest. Alan was the middle man and accepted a founder's fee.

Chuck and I returned to view our estate,

Further from the US border, changes in the countryside had become obvious for there were fewer people. Some telephone poles were tilted way over as if no one cared. The flat plains were "used for nothing," a local hitch hiker claimed. That attitude accommodated nature by leaving the marsh as it chose to be.

Alan and Alice's straight laces of hospitality accepted us into their home despite their temporary loss of privacy. The Black house, a singular structure, was perched atop a bare hill vulnerable to winds and weather, as tree nor protective landscape device arose in defense. That positioning allowed for unrestricted viewing of automotive approach from any direction. The wind punished the unheated bathroom and the disagreeable chemical toilet.

She and Alan were of another culture from us. Alice

had to atone her time to Alan when she was in the village. It became oppressive to hear their turn of the century interplay. She was a rebel in her own rite living where, as she called it, "Gossipy Tatamagouche." She said she did not care what people thought and so walked proudly. We were accepted with care as Jesus hanging on the wall assured. Alice and Alan were complex, so as not to complicate the relationship, we avoided straight talking politics and experimental proclivities.

One lane bridges startled and rattled as we approached our land. We were determined to sleep there, to waken in our place, clean from the rain and untrammeled by humans. A sloped mountain ascended, bright by moonlight, large and close to the horizon. Two side posts of an old gate remained as entry to an evergreen forest. They outlined a grassy field, spreading, rolling and turned flat with wind.

Down an incline lay remains of tumbled down barns and the nearly bare framework of a house. Personal emotions and external cognition were felt as we imagined hundred years past when builders and levers worked the growth, relocated boulders and planted crooked apple trees. The impending winds were evident for much had grown sidewise. Bare feet couldn't root through the thickness of the green carpet. Different from the sudden drops and cliff edged trails of familiar Vermont forests, our new place had a routinely flat aspect. It had been clear cut once for most trees were small in stature so recuperation would be a long time coming. I called it flat but only by contrast. Kansas is flat. This was nothing like Kansas. Our place on Spindle Hill spread high enough to spot the ocean and was that Prince Edward Island in the misty distance? This was to be our home.

Next came preparing for the move, packing our VW bus with bulk food and construction supplies. Tony Mathews, a Montague Farm cohort joined us adding glee. Tony was a smiling, singing, effervescent dead serious draft dodger or draft resister who maintained contact with his draft board to assure their knowing his intentions. The appellation, "Draft Resistor" or "War Tax Resistor" eventually became more favored terms preferable to the sneaky "Draft Dodger," to more ethically represent those who conscientiously refused to participate in machinations of war. I rather enjoyed the term dodger harkening back to the elusive antics of Charles Dickens' "Artful Dodger"[17] who exemplified cunning when confronted with opposition. But resistors re-identified how they wanted to be perceived.

Tony maintained communication with his California draft board so they would have access to his anti Viet Nam war statement, to update them to his whereabouts, almost as a challenge to his commitment as if proclaiming, "Try me!"

Surprise! Unexpected rejection at the Calais, ME border set us back.

We sat dormant as stones at that border queue and then in stagnant office air while hundreds of cars passed through. An angry man chased a woman, barged her bumper, ran along her driver's door and slapped her head. They were both admitted into Canada. Law abiding citizens and border patrol stared vacantly while our character was judged.

"Canada does not want people such as you!"

Understandable! We were draft dodgers.

The acreage purchased in Tatamagouche would have to wait for a more auspicious era when either Viet Nam had ended or a less defining appearance could slip us across the border. Our treachery, five long hairs, one nursing mother, another pregnant, a wooden keg of tamari, sacks of BROWN rice, oats and beans. You can see our patchwork.

"Who do they think they are, eating like the ol' days? Comin here as if we want them!"

"Unpack the van! step over there!"

Hours searching for contraband, splaying our possessions across the tarmac, weapons readily gripped in a militant stance. Individual interrogation went like this.

"Are you married?"

---

17   The Artful Dodger, Charles Dickens *Oliver Twist* 1838

"How long, where, when? And where is the license?
"Yes we are, by common law. We have been together for
years!"

"He said your marriage certificate was at your parents'
house. You lie. Canada doesn't want you. Turn around; pack
your stuff! Git!"

They never found the hunting rifle or the crushed
roach. Ha!

Rejection turned us back to the good ol US border
where paper factories were visibly and indifferently permitted to discharge poisons. Back toward Massachusetts!
Our woes nursed and relatively mild, were offset by digging
clams, picking wild blueberries and sleeping on the beach
along the magnificent coast. Would the tide be with us? A
disquieting siren disturbed the silence. Rocks ahead.

There followed days of indecision, melancholia and the
repetitious absurdities of life. Autumn felt more metaphys-
ical in its slow readying for winter, all things softly settling
into earth. In preparation for birth, I identified with longevity of root crops more resistant to decomposition.

We were invited to consider a match at the spacious
Montague Farm.

My first viewing of the farm featured Tony churning
butter on the thick granite New England front stoop while
sultry Laura sat nearby tricking her pup with a string to
chase its tail. Cathy was baking Irish soda bread in the wood
stove. No more macrobiotics for me. Cathy and Laz worked
industriously in their studio creating marbled paper and
binding books. Steven was most likely on the phone, a chore-
ographer of elaborate exchange. Sluggo was typing his devo-
tional history book and viewing the southerly sloping garden
from his swivel chair or climbing the hill to enact the limber-
ing twist-um exercise. Wonka could be heard tap dancing in
Marshall's barn room, her metal taps on wood resounding
throughout. Michael maneuvered kindly, cryptically and
professorially; tall congenial peaceful Marsden suddenly
appeared; charming Scotsman, Alex Kelly and Wilton, bridge
building engineer and astute son of an Australian diplomat
were there, all enjoying the ambience, so much of which

they generated. Everyone radiated political renegade. Blunt sadness underlay, for Marshall Bloom, commune brother and one of the geniuses of the 60's, had recently died, purposefully inhaling the fumes of his green Spitfire Triumph. Ironic car names for him! We did not yet suffer his loss personally, except by our newfound connections and resistance to what oppressed.

The house's original rooms included a "Birthing Room" and according to its derivation, was utilized that fall by Kathy and Laz giving birth to Noah in secular home birth methodology. The shallow Count Rumford fire place with refractory angled sides was designed for increased heat reflection. The unheated pantry with entry from the back of the house horrified with years of unnavigable clutter and likewise attracted me with possibility. I visualized storage shelves throughout. Capricorn orgasm, a friend called it. Upstairs offered private angles and recesses but the kitchen remained the prime magnet for what could materialize and ballast for what proved unsteady elsewhere. Decisively, we accepted the offer to move in.

The few women present would not be readily commandeered even though they often wore dresses. Not having to wear tight clothes depicted a different softer sexuality without advertising curves and crease. The clothing displayed clever embossed stitching and typical of early New England, calico. Vintage expressions were easily spotted at rummage sales or inexpensive thrift shops. The thin fabric did little to add discretion to nipples but assured cooler temperature and femininity. Janice and my cladding of thick denim and leather work boots had accommodated JP life. We adjusted comfortably.

Margaret at the sister farm, conscientious like a customizing tailor, picked abstemiously from her storeroom sized closet, hundreds of dresses all hanger hung, a historical ancestry of farmers' wife or debutante. One frock she was able to part with became my occasional farm dress. It draped sinuously when tiresome work clothes were shed. The dress matched the soda bread, the carraway seeds and the rolling pin biscuits.

We were not drifters or jocks. What came out of mouths were topics swelling in cigarette smoke minus locker room splat. No silly pitched voices. We were newly defined stereotypes. Smart, serious, educated and somewhat like men, though not in smell or the way we walked in this era of resistance and toward what we viewed as progress.

Secure space in my bedroom supplied me with yin yang: comfort, confusion, first baby born, hopeful knocks on the door, passion and pain, and curious revelations about body parts and performance. Music above, voices below. Sometimes laughter sounds like hysterical crying.

"I know who it is."

The new year of 1971 was almost upon us. Was it the beginning or the end? It was a day of putting on and taking off boots. I was nine months pregnant and on the cusp of delivery. The kitchen throbbed with peanut butter cookies and no left over salad. The kitty rolled her pretty piebald belly up for rubbing. Chuck played rough house, covering her eyes with a perverse hand. I put her out. We couldn't have degenerate cats too! My brother's visits continued to fill the barn with full mellow breath of his tenor sax. I did not dream of him because our interaction was untrammeled. My dreams instead were penetrated by what disturbed, like how challenging it was to understand, let alone pursue and receive love.

The dancing of dive bomber recluse flies directed my consideration to them, their goal, to die while tormenting. All else was still in the house until wakeful, shuffling footsteps, hot water streaming into the milk pail to cleanse teats before milking, and then the rooster's unyielding crow.

Tony in the Prime Seat

Who was in the prime seat, the fat wooden rocker next to the cook stove? Someone usually claimed what "first come" provided. Even the wild man, John Miller from "The Ranch" down Chestnut Hill Road, took his turn smiling, sipping and chawing the fat with anyone. I tended to ignore hanger-oners. What was the chat? I sometimes did not care or relax for long. I toted, chopped, ground flour and concentrated on my pregnant body.

I eventually obtained a ground floor two room suite facing east and south. The back bedroom was compact and gifted with a skinny closet. The front room was for my invaluable desk, bay window plants, an unmanageable wood stove for incipient fire making skills and eventually, for my child's space. Janice had added a rustic wallpaper with a pattern repeating itself as if down one lane and back or towards something calm and homey. A scene of soft leafed trees suggested rural entry to where one belonged. That rustic road pattern became a metaphor of arrival and departure.

Seasonally, the crickets were so raucous, the air was thick with rhythmic unrelenting insect expression, cacophonous on the occasion when their communication persisted, especially loud when I retreated to my open window room. One nomad had hopped its way over the sill. "Crick, crick crick crick crick," broke the quiet. But in silence, you could hear the brook way down the hill where bubbles composited into one flowing sound. The differential between day and night influenced expansion and contraction. Warped floor boards shrank and wavered. Mid night, creek creek creeking filled your ears with no fear, of whathaunted before you. Jimmy Carter was honest to reveal what he feared most, being lost in the woods. I knew what he meant by that total dissolution. Some can read mental magnetic maps towards their goal. Some read moss on the north face of trees. Others feel the pulse of the planet and notice buds and grasses that change overnight. Others smell the air and cannot pass treated city water over their lips nor pass by blossoms without exclamation.

The commune was very young so the inhabitants had not figured out everything about rural living. We did just fine milking, eating together like farm families of old and innovating family life. We had incompletely seasoned wood doubly defeated by many angles in the stove pipe. Who harvested the firewood anyway from our deep woods? I knew little of identifying qualities of trees, dead, dry and seasoned, fallen and wet, deciduous or evergreen. Without cord wood consciousness, there were no choices. Instead, there was unspoken gratitude for those who provided any fuel. The stacks in the woodshed were picked over to avoid leaked on chunks, selecting what might produce more than smoke.

In my front room, I constructed a tool closet, subordinately accessible under the living room steps. Ingenious creation that! By removing the plaster and lathe, conniving shelves from reject lumber and fitting a slender door, I organized myself with simple essentials, my own few tools in an organized place right off my bedroom. I saved myself from being pissed off while searching for the right size screwdriver and I flourished learning tools. I commiserated with those who couldn't afford tools or learn how to repair what was simply broken.

Keeping the commune automotive fleet in gear was someone else's inheritance. Trucks, vans, and of course the omnivorous cars. I donated my Philadelphia van which soon "ran itself" silly and dead. We usually named the vehicles which assumed personalities reflecting the owner: Bruffy, Cosmo, The Chuckbus, Mighty Might, Josephine, Flash, Peewee. We had a Hudson grinning wide. I learned the maneuvers of a tractor, our Farmall A, in order to understand and join in the mechanical field work that absorbed the men. Its front stabilizing wheels were not close together like the majestically fearful M which left one wondering about tip and crush. Tractors assured us of larger agricultural efforts: to spread manure, plow, harrow, disc, utilize the planter for an acre or more of field corn. And of course, haying.

We undertook large agricultural operations in consort with our sister farm in Wendell. Our Organic Truck optimistically transported surplus to Amherst where we peddled vegetables. Aspiring to provide feed corn for our cows, it was arranged that we swab out a season's worth of schloop from the Whippoorwill Chicken Farm in North Leverett. Being on that crew is where I met DW, Daniel Whittemore Keller. We shoveled into wheelbarrows, the capable farmer's friend, rolled down corridors to the ramp, below which awaited the shit spreader. Dump! Resume! Dump and so on until brimming the load, then trundle down to Moores Corners, where currently resides the Leverett Food Co-op, but then a few acres of scrabby field, hungry recipient for our applications. That terrible whirring spreader machine did its job but likewise sprayed onto the driver's unimpressed back. In the heat of the day, on the ragged up hill battle to refuel, I balanced on the metal hitch and held securely to D, absorbing the power of his lean frame against my chest and accepting the pleasure of first impact, our intimacy atypically thus tainted.

Sam and Janice constructed a 10x10 corn crib to season shucked cobs for winter feed. If the small gage chicken wire was secure, it repelled mice and crows and the crib was proud in its accomplishments. Golden yellow cobs. A crib full of them. A means was devised to connect a tractor's power take off (a PTO) to turn gears that rolled a long conveyor belt that cranked grinders that ground the corn into the makings of silage. Think of Charlie Chaplin in the film "Modern Times "and you can visualize our interactive positions, cogs and gears. The machine whistled and shot pulverized corn arcing out the funnel, dusting the air with color, bits of kernel and cob and sifting silage material down onto a massive pile to be carted to the smaller recipient silo where it could ferment into a delectable cow mash according to desired temperature and ideal tending. How long had that empty silo sniffed for content? This lesser silo was about 6 ft diameter. It took conscientious monitoring to assure correct balance of moisture and heat or the off kilter sour slurry was hard to take! It was hard to take!

The other silo was a wooden beauty, approximately 15 ft diameter, with an incomplete circular roof deranged by time and into which weather and rhyme entered. It was coated and decayed and made merry with bird nests and drips.

After fertile broody hen[18] eggs hatched, I lobbed the undeveloped sulfurous ones, to splat them explosively against the far wall. I stood at the opening, peering from that second story cow barn, across which I flung my folly. Explosive matter fell to effervesce. I was probably fueling the rats.

---

18   Broodie hens will set on a clutch of eggs for 21 days. If fertile, eggs will hatch. Not all hens go broodie for it has been bred out by hybridization. Hatching is replaced by electric incubators.

LIVING WITH ANIMALS

I became a chicken lady. My avian instincts awakened. Those perfect eggs, the ones I could collect before a wayward egg eater ravaged them, were a gorgeous warm oval in the hand. The chickens complemented our interests with linguistics for they could sing operatic refrain. They had so much to communicate. "I laid an egg" or "Me first," or "Come see what I found," or "Yahoo I sing, I sing," or "Alert, alert! a hawk," or "I go to roost," or it was time to quietly "Cheep, cheep" under the wing.

Living with animals added security, meaning, anatomy lessons, and symbiosis. There were deep hefty smells in the barn with Dolly, the horned Jersey cow of moony fluid eyes. Or big boned Guernsey Delilah or Burmie the bull or Adelia, the Charolais of pale mauve grey. The cows comforted with their bulk and heat and allowed a milker to lean into their flank and breathe in their heady cow hide or defrost cold fingers anywhere.

Dogs added simpatico and devotion. But cats challenged impatient dog lovers to not expect doggie devotion and to accept their more estranged manner. Cats loved independently and unexpectedly. And who is that rubbing against my leg? It is Mama Cat or Beeps come to get her share. She opens her dainty mouth and a direct single stream of hot milk shoots right in. When she tires of the feat, she licks meticulously and is content for nap or hunt.

I bonded to that trim cat of many colors in one tortoise shell pattern accented by duplicate white splotches under her eye cheeks that bounced as she walked. "Beep. Beep. Here I come. Beep." Anna had once collected Beeps from the vet, stopped to visit a friend and overlooked kitty's stealthy presence under the car seat. "No Beeps!" "Where is Beeps?" I sped to town and resounded my "Kitty, kitty, kitty-kitty-kitty" refrain over and over undefeatedly calling into the neighborhood and "What? Do I hear her up in that tree, forlorn and yet meow hopeful?" She was returned to her rightful place and now stands religiously at her dairy bar squirt, squirt!

How raunchy and rank was the barn with its prevailing
inhabitants, chickens, cows and of course sneaky wild things.
Deep within the cow and muffled by multiple bulky rumbles,
lie the interior workings of digestion. She reverberates and
pleasantly belches raw grass; her nostrils splay. From fresh
grass or dry hay alone, upheaval progresses. Sizeable flat
molars grind and pulverize into pulp, to prized cow paddy, to
milk or to meat. Astounding!

She-cow

Conceive of this cow
      whose head bulks more than your chest
who'd rather stay in the belly of the barn than graze in
pasture
fresh
Horse flies gnaw voracious from her steam
She rids herself of pesky flies the size of wasps
      sucking through hide she can whap with her accurate
tail
She's lashed me when so moved
Her nose whips back to score an unprotected itch
      like our own backs we can no longer reach

Her heat speaks volumes
Beware, recoil from shifting hooves
and willingly scrub cow slathers
Great wonderful cow beast
Human enough in some ways, yes

I open the door and she, great mastodon of the barn
Converses moo-speech to my presence
I'll brush her and she melts
      accepting exploration on the nether world of teats
Those perfectly pendulous tubes fit my woman-hands
      or the insistent suck of her kind

Egad! She pees! I pull my boot from urine that makes me
throaty
      a deep musk does penetrate the air
      it spreads a puddle seeking cracks in aged cement
She lies on stanchion piles deep and saturate
The top fresh, loosely knit
      hay once tasty as a field of grass
That big head
What does she think
Her conscious cow considerations like our own

BIRTHING

The barn, a dosimeter of comfort and belonging, was a place to leave human interaction to itself. The house with pulse and histories was lure, but the few steps out to the garden or barn with animals and reverent smells, its compost heaps in reciprocal cycle, was elemental.

The smells of the barn were different near the grain bin where the air tasted of molasses mixed into the dairy mash. Fifty pound burlap sacks were so fragrant you could almost be nourished by breathing. Not so with carnal smelling pet food. We had ravenous farm dogs but not like those banded wildly together at the JP where their owners, who also did not belong, madly rushed the front door in a pack of distorted psyches.

Dogs, usually willing to come near for the hand to stroke cushy fur, were always anxious for food, their lips lathering in anticipation. They were punctual at meal time but devoid of etiquette to rule who came first at either bowl. Drooling, then wanton devouring, they skipped the chewing for the whole immediacy of animal nature.

Dog gulps were unlike the delicate mouthing of cats who picked precisely through the bits as they crunched methodically, their mouths instantly turned cruel if trespassed upon. The several barn cats peered in wait for what's to come, nudging purrs against each other in me first insistence.

"Gimme a kiss. A kiss. No? Oh! OK. That was cheap."

All the animals were ready at first light for breakfast from a willing barn hand. They lined up near the grain bin where the sizeable bags of scoopy kibble always threatened to be empty, but had survived gnawing incursions of likewise hungry rodents. Creature presence was evident in the worn carpentry of the bin, seams bedeviled with widened tell tale optimistic holes which incited mice and sizeable rats from unreachable crannies behind the planks. They reamed the cracks which became a door.

On the milking stool an olfactory temperament was favored. Most milk cows routinely stood, stately, peaceful and permissive while milkers rubbed and brushed and pulled down teats and drained the udder in milky passage. Delilah displayed a different recalcitrance and you knew and were prepared to be repeatedly wapped by her tail which she pretended was a swish to ward off the flies. I tied her pride to her rear leg! All this we city folk learned, mastered and adored. It was revealing to see our cool hand Stevie D, the suave lady's man, return from the barn aglow with bovine company.

Team Work and Teachers

Trucks, cars and tractor engines were rebuilt and the almighty brake job along with lesser skilled jobs of changing oil or tires. The spiraling energy within a generator and a coil, the previously arcane sequencing of an engine, were explained. I observed reusing parts as teacher, master mechanic and kind generous friend, Steve Sayer, reconstructed motors. I called him Doctor or Seance, for he was guru and farm magician. He trusted himself enough to oversee my carburetor rebuild and brake job. He orated me through logistics of rewiring lamps; many needed attention.

I did not want to be typically in the kitchen or garden. When Chris and John visited, John recognized need as opportunity and helped me construct The Chicken Hilton, a grand stand-up-in chicken hotel with a southern facing picture window. He taught me how to use a saw correctly. "Don't press it down. Let the saw cut for you!"

I gophered when he helped me cement blocks to form a double binned 5x8 ft outhouse composting repository adjacent to the artistic outhouse.

These were no longer trim city girl hands. They had matured into my ancestral White Russian stone mason hands, muscled, blocky and sure. They belonged convincingly on a cow or shifting stones. My maiden name Finestone, was somehow acquired at Ellis Island, for Grandpop was not a jeweler nor even a mason yet, but rather a "yeshivah bocher," a student at a Jewish school as far as scant family history goes. He became a mason in Philadelphia, first a hireling, then strategizing how to hire himself, and then contracting the construction of the common brick and stone row homes.

All of us left the boundaries of the farm to drive miles to mow, rake, bale and transport thousands of hay bales into the three tiers of our historical barn, the top tier being high off ground level. Those hay days brought us together as a crew that could get big farming done. The fresh fragrance of new mown hay filled the air with food

like a fragrance so full that one forgot to be hungry for people food.

The barn was one of the wonders of historical architec-
ture as beams spanned wide within the 70 x 30 foot main
structure. The additional side cow barn lined with metal
stanchions, was half that again. Standing in the main nave
one felt the actuality of ancestral carpenters wielding ham-
mers to impale flat iron nails and masterfully centering
yellow pine beams directly over connecting pins. Our crew
flourished, proved to be able and strong and like the old
days, learned grace with hayforks after only once impaling a
prong into my foot.

Dawn peaked the eastern Ripley hill and glazed my
face, especially my face, in the warm enough bed. It became
natural to crave sunrise. Blessed brightness paved the way
for much to come, to rise, to get to it. Ah! It was so cold but
we were young, inexperienced and resilient. We embraced
the notion of hardy farmers. Must start the fires, feed the
kids, milk the cows, liberate the hens...

Then spring challenged.

Haying, roofing the barn, the garden gorgeous with
what did you call it? Celeriac? Can't we just grow celery?

Ah! The decades of splendid barn clutter. Vast open
spaces with storage, animal stalls, a room for mechanics, hay
lofts, silos, even a side room for what had been milk process-
ing. New England collections and hippie discard were dis-
gorged over generations. Tires, bald, but could they be useful
for, for, what? A swing? And rags, too many. Save those for
the car shop; and before town hazardous waste collection
days, old crank case oil for rusty blades, caution! toxic! Tin
cans, metal shafts, nuts and bolts, cartons of papers caved in
sideways, farm dereliction in stalls coated with dried chaff
and poop. Cracked buckets. They're metal! and so useful for
tag sale collections of nuts and bolts. "Take me for a dollar if
you please!" Cartons with no sustenance, leather farm
regalia piled in stalls which once housed small animals. Utility of ancient chaff scraped into ah yes, a usable
wheelbarrow, and shape shifted towards the garden. And
items of traditional pragmatics, a four foot diameter circular

saw blade hung artistically on the side of the barn, its big teeth grinning into the future and defending a goose pen enclosure admired by leaf peepers. "Oh look honey. It's a pig!" "Hey lady! That is a goose!"

Some clever Yankee had discovered, unearthed and dragged massive flat boulders and positioned them to fashion the most solid stairway for cow access from lower to upper barn, from pasture to stanchion. Reputedly, even the cows were sure footed enough to hazard the climb to the "milking parlor," a genteel nomenclature. There you enter a long open space lined with part wooden part metal s tanchions for controlled milking positions where once dozens of dairy cows manually released their flows. Now our cows clomped into position up less threatening ramps and respectfully, in anticipation of milking rituals, slid their wide necks into the clever controlling stanchion and awaited feed, hay, brushing and washing of their compromised teats and bag, dusty and worse from lying on sometimes tainted ground. Leaning in to the fragrant hide of a complacent cow who had rather enjoyed the brush massage, warming stiff fingers on her hot body, these were experiences that assured love of place and relationship with her grand bovine body.

The corner of the barn sheltered an unused two-seater, an in, not out-house. From its long vacated seats, one could peer into the lower depths of the barn where time had attended to dissolution and on nearby pegs, drooped the dusty pea coat attributed to the hired hand who fell to his death onto a pitchfork. Save the pitchfork! Leave the coat in place. I was down cellar tapping cider and there he creepy was, discordantly standing to hide behind the pillar, stiff and discreet, stiff I say for his spine was the pillar and his black coat and brimmed hat embraced the wood. I scrammed up the cellar stairs and leaned shut the door. Smokey looked at me and said, "What! Ph! Oh! You saw him!"

Some people believe in afterlife, spirit world, ghosts. I had inherited a Jewish belief to accept no other gods and so was not prone to accept the reality of the unknown. But when the he of the coat sneaked in on me and keen iciness did enter the room, I knew something different. I had been washing my hair at the kitchen sink. The pantry room door swung in on clever hinges, inching one way and then the other, but it had not swung back into place. I was alone in the house. No one answered my call. The door swung in, stayed put, swung open and stilled.

"How dare you come in on me. I have soap in my eyes! Get out!"

The framework of New England, the vein of HP Lovecraft, was in the neighborhood. As were "door knob" spiders, those cushy blobs of body big as a knob. Smokey would tease with them as he had inherited no fear of creatures big or small. He lobbed one at me which hit repulsively with its no bone juice and tattooed my shoulder. Smokey taught me how to safely grab a snake, if I ever wanted to, one hand behind the head and the other hand holding firm the writhing body so it would not pee on me. Yes, I've done it to prove some concept of mettle, but with the "friendly" local garter snake, yet my heart did leap.

Wood Lover's Mantra

Our chainsaw artists, Tony and Sam, supplied us with firewood. They scoured the forest for dead trees or they dissected those encroaching upon preferred stands. I call them artists because felling a large tree entails acute observation and skill. Massive trunks threaten to fall in the wrong direction or to unpredictably split and so, decapitate. How rapturous to hear the crack, the splintering of a tree and to have it fall as planned, between and not onto its neighbor where it would hang inaccessibly and threateningly high. Novices were up to that protracted laborious task.

Unless you choose to leave a forest on its own, unaffectedly wild, then long range planning enhances forests destined for fire wood, maple sugar bush or to ensure diversity.

Dry wood does not mean seasoned wood. Seasoned wood has had one to two years to lie before burning so the pervasive sap evaporates. Then stacking undercover prevents rain seeping in. Green wood smolders and produces dread creosote, that black combustible crusty soot inside a chimney and the cause of many a fire.

Understanding Btu's of cord wood does not provide decent firewood, especially for those not born under the stars of wood heat. Seasoned firewood is logically and optimally hotter and safer. But those guys rejoiced in big forest.

Many people never experience that vast rich presence of trees, inhalations of natural decay and growth, the release of oxygen which makes sure we continue to live. It is a spiritual place. "I welcome you into my temple."

Once, a chimney fire ignited in our house. The roar raised the rafters. Sleepers ran from rooms in state of disarray, focused only on salvation. While we crazily doused and remedied, an unfavored guest sat on the sofa and threw the I Ching to see what it all meant. Roger the Dodger he was called. The raging flames were extinguished by smothering the fire in the stove and spraying from the roof down into the flue. We then had to consider the state of the overly heated old bricks. Sleep was elusive that night and until the chimney was approved by the "chimney doctor."

We can guffaw at our young selves who cut and tried to burn those damn logs. "Hey, it was wood wasn't it?" That was what we had and that was who we were until we organized what we understood better.

After felling and sawing into three to four-foot sections, those sectioned logs would be carted to where the saw of poetic injustice, the hungry cordwood buzz saw, a 4 foot diameter blade with shark teeth, was belted to the power-take-off, the PTO, which transmitted the surge of the tractor engine around a substantial metal structure that turned a wide belt which rotated the blade. Logs would be positioned on the hinged shelf that tipped into the whirring blade, lethal as Robert Frost knew with one faulty misstep, "Out Out."[19] Shrill keening of the cut through solid wooden matter, might have been enough to keep the senses on high alert. Whir, zzzzzzzzzping and it is neatly done, slicing through one more segment to split, stack, carry in and tend, to assure up close heat for ideal utility and comfort.

What ruthless entity that threatening mechanism proved. It preceded the next tantric task of splitting hunks to stove size. Chuck and Steve Marsden thrived with repetitions of balance, assuring shins were not in the way of rebound, positioning the awkward chunk, raising the axe with a strong arm to swing down to hear that rewarding crack if it was oak. Or if the grainwas knotty or whorled, a groan of resistance.

When the chimney required biannual attention, we were the chimney sweeps, one who climbed the roof, one in the cellar who peered via a mirror inserted in the bottom trap to observe sooty accumulation. The makeshift reamer of coiled chicken wire was inserted with a lengthy top and bottom rope, one person pulling up, one pulling down cough cough hack hack and cover your nose until the inside avenue of the flue was visible, cleared of flammable creosote to reveal straight brick shaft.

The stove required regular cleaning too. Ignitable ashes would cool in tin containers unless a lazy scooper preferred to toss it onto the property and burn down the house. This

---

19   Robert Frost poem "Out Out" Young lad loses hand. Disaster!

organic ash was free fertilizer to nourish and alkaline the Northeast's acid soil.

Cut once, warm twice is the wood lover's mantra.

Farm Challenges

Challenge, the human condition in every family, farm, wee apartment or sprawling estate. A naughty pet, the headstrong herd, a rural mailbox ruined by delinquent drive-by batting practice. Meal worms, the tread of boots, an ajar storm door, a welcome-in torn mosquito screen. Well rise and shine, like it or not. Animals and kids prioritize the hour.

Collect weeds for the chickens to supplement bought grain. Pull the carrot, listen to its resistant thlunk as it yields its vegetarian roots, rub off a bit of soil and bite. Carotene your spirit. One minute seed produces a cabbage bouquet red or green and parsley, curled or flat.

Grow your own and animal food, food like zucchini too thick skinned to penetrate with a kitchen knife, zucchini as large as boats no one knew how to cook, but proud at the Franklin County Fair. Locate cabbage worms hiding in the core. Racoons, woodchucks, porcupine, deer, rampaging pigs and escaped cows, weak fences, drought and flood. Weeds only look different from seedlings to an undistracted eye. "What? He pulled the carrots? Goddamn!"

The delight of kneeling undisturbed in the garden, captured me. Soil is clean dirt. "Love Among the Cabbages," was a chapter in a book by Cleve Baxter, ex- CIA interrogator who tested sensory perception in plants. We tested his theory in our own scratchy way, to see if plants related well to human passion and saw no discernible difference except between the mashed down rows. The pleasure did not outweigh the discomfort.

The genetic power and promise of each seed was discrete and different as siblings. The inherited ragamuffin collection of old seed packets did not always produce as advertised. Age took its toll and fertility dissipated the promise. Too many seeds dropped in one row created a ghetto. Spacing, timing, nourishment and water requirements were fundamentals.

Oh shit on my foot and oh shit, here come the kids! My darlings. My life. Look Eben. A worm! a balm for impatience.

"A vern, a vern!" occupied him and then as commander, he
was on my lap.

A chicken will eat a person if you lay still long enough. The
flock of recalcitrant chickens, were they really hens? Where were
the promised eggs? "Got them cheap!" Half of the cannibalized
crowd were roosters. The females, traumatized by relocation,
were further inhibited by rats or regulated by old age. I salvaged
a damp bag of compacted cement and ignored admonitions to
buy new. Mix, spray and cram the grit into tunnel holes. I navigated the fruitlessness of pre-dampened mortar by trying to
save money. As predicted having once been moistened, it could
not set. Vermin regained subterranean access, or merely as they
pleased, through the entry that hung no door!

It was time to rid ourselves of geriatric birds. That first
butchering coincided with one of my parents' illustrious visits.
Butchering was directed by books and those free step by step
USDA pamphlets. Janice and I had been told to just, and when
you hear that word "just," it is time to just be on the alert! Just
hold the body and chop off the head and there you are! Even after the pathetic idiom of running around like a chicken without
its head made literal sense, we still had to pluck, gut and cook
for hours til edible, that old bird. Mom was adept at plucking
and singeing pin feathers, quality control from her thrifty family.

I walked to the barn nightly to tuck the chickens in. The
excess roosters had met their maker while hens involuntarily,
meticulously, dutifully, rhythmically, plucked at grit until the
lactating racoon plundered. We responded to mayhem with a
Dead-Eye-Dick bullet and attempts to do right by the sparse
summer pelt. Sad milky breasts were revealed. Intentions.
Resistance. Rueful death!

Several of us were milkers, a chore structured twice daily.
Typewriter fingers adapted and we sprouted bulbous thumb

muscles. Milk does not wait for fools nor did excess gallons. We delivered to raw milk neighbors and therefore met characters. Rodney lived intimately with his animals, an emotionally reciprocal relationship. "Come in!" he would gloriously chant from his perch, lying next to dogs, cats, pig, goat.... "Don't mind the mess. Your bottle is in the sink and the change too." I did mind his so called "mess" for the jug was cruddy despite the agreement. He was eccentrically upbeat and offered fair exchange in his reuse department of salvaged doors and windows and picturesque tales.

So what to do with excess milk? There is perplexity in making cheese. Boursin was the easiest because in a few days it was ready with garlic and salt masking off flavor. Yogurt and cottage cheese were simple, but not our stabs at hard cheese via USDA brochures. Imagine 2-3 gallons of milk per day taunting your fridge and self-sufficiency. I salvaged wide pine boards and constructed a multi shelved cheese closet in the back room but wax coating did not discourage mold nor mice.

CIDER

The back of our truck was piled with apples, free-for-the-clean-up of orchard drops. We celebrated on the 20 foot high cider press at PC, run by hydraulic tractor pulleys. Twenty of us at geared positions reminiscent again of Charlie Chaplin. Mom and Dad were present for the pressing. They commended specific processes in our life style. The stream of cider made sense as could living with strangers. "I wish I could join you in the steam bath but I'm too shy. At least your mom and I have lots to talk about on the drive home. Unlike the way she cried all the way home from the JP."

MOM BAKING

Mom baked bread in the wood oven and Dad carried on kneeling on the good earth or with whatever work the Boys were up to.

A note to Mom and Dad of things to remember after their departure:

*Dad forgot his work pants
*The ACLU periodical you brought is interesting

COMMUNITY CONFLICT

Some committed foes, a few regular coconspirators colonizing the counter at Lee Lund's general store, were out to "get us." There was a collection of signatures on a petition to confront us somehow.

Steven's brother Mark, incognito, photographer, Nikoned the counter top document. There was much ado about nothing we knew how to do, during that time of public discontent.

Midwifery was illegal in Massachusetts so we chose delivery at the nearest hospital, The Farren, a Catholic institution. We were not prejudiced. The nuns shaved and enema-ed me and officials threatened to not release our newborn because we had no name on the birth certificate.

"Can't put a name when you haven't named your baby!"

Social services sent Mrs. Cahill, an officious busy body to see when we were going to pay the bill. We claimed we were going to do just that! After inane back and forth and Chuck's telling her it was our business and demanding that she get out of our house, he stood up, dispersed a hot, reasonable enough explosive request that she leave. She resisted, he slammed his fist on the table and ordered again that she depart. "Get out of my house, Old Lady." That did it! An hour later, an officer arrived to hand us charges: Chuck for assault, which means to put the fear in someone's mind that you might hurt them. Me, for lewd and lascivious behavior, having a baby out of wedlock. We procured and compensated an up to date lawyer, the approachable judge was peeved to be bothered by an outmoded statute in Massachusetts, charges were dismissed, we paid minor court fees and entertained ourselves with another not unexpected outrage.

Too Risky a Business

Having not seen my family for long months, I decided to hitchhike from Mass to Philadelphia despite the possibilities. The surprise entry at Mom and Dad's back door was worth it. My infant would be secured against my chest in a carrier. "Surprise!" I could not suppress desire to share the wonder of a baby, a most sensational accomplishment.

What are the motives of drivers who acknowledged outstretched thumbs? I peered in to assess the façade. He was mid aged, suited and the passenger seat was clean. Inadequate as a gauge of character but ready to roll, I stowed my pack behind and transformed into his passenger. Stories of violence to women and ill-advised hitchhikers were tabloid headliners but I was on the road.

"Where can I take you?"

"Philadelphia."

"Not quite, but get in as far as..."

His droning soliloquy obscured the next half hour. I watched his profile for signs of temperament. Tightness intensified his forehead. He was drastically pissed. Doubtless a difference about government policy in Viet Nam or nuclear!

"Fuckin commie! I'm a patriot!"

I spy his unhealthy tongue. How much clearer could the warning signal have been? I have no use for his trash. Still, I continue to clarify the definition of patriotism. Definitions need defense.

"Me too! I love our constitution. Especially freedom of speech."

"You belong on the gallows, baby and all, not soiling my seat. You sort are trying to control my life."

The air in the compartment is too close. At home, Peter refers to me as "the nose that knows."

"OK I get it. Let me out the next stop."

"Proven fact! You commies are wrong."

"What about?"

"The Constitution. I have the arms here to prove it."

He indicated by solicitously patting his own bicep and the compartment under his seat then careening from the left lane to a dead stop half onto the median strip.

"Get out bitch!" and I was ejected into traffic left and right on the artery. I grabbed my pack even as he peeled out while decorating the air with his fist then middle finger. He'd show me, dirty, commie, hairy, hippy chick.

I knew my folly. Not dirty but imprudent! Had known it before. Still, diversions and risk taking were worth some drama.

My baby nursed and dreamed of secure fetal pressure. As an adult, he would admonish me for disregarding boundaries. An incredulously sympathetic driver deposited me at the family driveway, a pavement that led to reasonably stupefied adults.

The Bust

We were soon thereafter busted. Building inspector, Frank Dudek, a florid character, was on the prowl, skulking to find ways to harass and eliminate our perceived threat to his community. "Aha!" He found it! One illegal potted plant in a terra cotta container dull from mineral scaling which coated its sides like what plasters the planet. But nature knows no boundaries nor do rebels in mundane acts of rebellion. "One little dope plant."

That potted marijuana plant on a window ledge was spotted by the eagle eye and accordingly, Dudek and company barged into the Garden Apartment where Robison was lazing in private afternoon haze. With documents in hand, they confiscated for testing, every herb on the kitchen shelf, as the Simon and Garfunkel song goes "parsley, sage, rosemary and thyme" never to be seen again, even for culinary endeavors. They arrested Tony in lieu of an accountable head of household.

Subsequently, the Board of Health proceeded to serve us with documented transgressions like an electric socket not being so many inches above or beyond or as required, elsewhere. All effects were itemized and we were designated to be a boarding house. That meant we were subject to a restricted number of residents, not more than six or so, unrelated by blood or marriage, and therefore not permitted to live together unless legitimized by the town. We laid low for a while and without more ado, wondered if the town found other issues more pressing?

Politics and Religion

After Marshall Bloom's death, this excerpt from his writings, a logical reaction to a world gone askew, was found in the barn:

"We are people who have traveled about a bit and now find ourselves here, where chaos stops at our border and Nature's order and unity may begin... We are here to do our will, and Nature's will, and seek a special unity of our hearts, minds, bodies, homes, trees and river... We are pretty boy floyd[20] associates, banded together as outlaws and renegades against that which is said to be lawful in the eyes of some. Our standards are our own or those of all times..."

Marshall was one of the founders of our farm and LNS, Liberation News Service. As an alternative press journalist, he was a notorious young wonder of the 60's, active in Jewish youth movements, a civil rights activist in more than theory by participating in voter registration in Selma, AL.

Marshall was influential at Amherst College, as a dorm advisor, on the school newspaper, amid political foes and peers. Decades later, at an Amherst College reunion, one veteran retrospectively lauded him for being his most trusted correspondent while stationed in Viet Nam. Marshall maintained pure loyalty and love for that veteran who had chosen the military while Marshall had been antithetically on a road of resistance. He staged a walkout of his 1966 Amherst graduation with Elliot Eisenberg and other persons unknown to me, for Robert McNamara, Secretary of Defense under Kennedy, was the keynote speaker. McNamara was renowned for escalating the war and bombing attacks exceeding military posts which incurred huge civilian casualties. Marshall foreclosed receiving his Amherst College diploma publicly by staging that protest in a Blue Blood American place of respect, dignity and diplomacy.

---

20   Capital letters unknown in original Marshall document

Later, at London School of Economics, Marshall's antics and anti Vietnam organizing led to expulsion during a tumultuous time of his and the school's political life.

Much later, Sluggo debated Westmoreland at a college forum. Daniel chose to plow the Wendell field rather than attend Amherst graduation, to the dismay of his parents.

LNS tales and personal histories elicited nods and guffaws, flitted or cemented our "trough." Life without brother Marshall had to be conceivable.

Opportunity and reason had it that we JP expatriates, commune sorts who had likewise suffered grievously were invited to fill the ranks.

"We are down a few" was one explanation.

Our life style was a political statement but we were superficially known except for Chuck who had ventured toward PC's conversational space. It was unusual for The Montague Farm Commune to be so receptive for they were not blindly seeking members. They were sympathetic, we were appealing, had a baby and were receptive to their diversified styles despite being more indoors. They were also cunningly experimental as artists, journalists, historians, book binders, all relaxing into the bosom of a real farm.

The dominant culture included the seasonal Christmas tree. Mostly there was zero interest in traditional religion, it being "the opiate of the people."[21]

Buddhism replaced religious inheritance for some and succored the place where tradition did once reside. Some fastidiously chose astrology, pursued healers, spiritualists or Kundalini Yoga. I brought a very basic Jewish ritual to the household with my Chanukah menorah, so my son would see my family way, a modicum of balance in the Christian world. When the pigs were introduced to the farm, I chose to not care but accepted a role in tending them. Pigs would never have been my animal of choice but I was living with

---

21   Karl Marx warned that political and social needs were sublimated when the masses prayed for religious release rather than rally for change

pork eaters and I accepted flock and herd. Smart pigs! They retreated to the far end of their pen to deposit.

Being a religious minority was familiar and hardly uncomfortable with open minded thinkers. The wild disregard of racist Pastor Flogi (sp) who dropped by to save our souls was met with unflappable reproach to his lurking racism. He referred to quotes from his Bible how "all Negroes should be returned to Africa" and me, a Jew, would soon see truth and salvation from Jesus my savior.

Few Blacks or other people of color resided in Franklin County. Two notables were Wally and Juanita Nelson, practiced, renowned, committed pacifists and war tax resisters who helped train us in preparation for anti nuclear civil disobedience. There was one Black gentleman on Sam's later civil disobedience jury trial and two activists in Turners Falls who helped organize a unifying of community in support of minority neighbors. "If you are white, you are a racist!" the Black organizer inexpertly and prematurely proclaimed. Interesting opinion! His pronouncement further divided rather than propel us toward a coordinated action.

Our table was animated by seeking ways to score cash, relaying of data about national or farm debts and deals, critiquing of politics and people and at the 7 o'clock ritual news hour, cheering or jeering. "It's time for Walter." We cringed the mounting count of war dead. Ron Kovic's book, *Born on the Fourth of July*, 1976, opened hearts and minds to the plight of American soldiers. Within the Black Panther vanguard there was governmental murder. The 1968 Democratic National Convention gassed and kicked us in the groin and Kent State killed our own. While war smoldered, we struggled with universals like security, cohabitation and crafting our newborn family. We were having babies, getting high, working hard and mostly enjoying our lives. Mixed smoke smudged the air above the chimney. We chose our form of pollution. Revolution was a state of mind and a life style. What complicated times! The Vietnamese were not our enemies.

I received a publication wrapped in plain brown paper. The guarded postmaster itched in wondering or peeking within. It was the publication from The Weather Underground, *Osawatomie*. A friend from Philadelphia was in that organization and had heard of Sam's NO NUKES civil disobedience action. He sent me their media rag, an intimacy from an overtly covert source for I knew the radical activist had reservations about the priority of environmental as
opposed to social action.

We were glibly Pretty Boy Floyd, the name painted on our out front RFD (rural free delivery) mailbox an
expression of rebellious identity. Floyd had been a notorious bank robber in the 1930's, a Robin Hood type character who destroyed mortgage documents, freeing working poor from bank debt. Then we evolved into The Montague Farmers as death, birth, agriculture and animals redefined us. Other town farmers did not object to our name as far as we knew and we were not challenging their rightful claim.

There were many of us so there was minimal time to deeply develop peripheral friendships. We mostly interacted with our sister communes, PC aka Packer Corners and
Wendell, aka The Duel, where we were related by college, a band, intimacies and agriculture in our grow your own constituency. Sex, drugs, rock and roll of course, but now you must add the farm.

Bob Rodale Jr of organic gardening fame, came with Ira for a visit. He really "dug" us and so gifted us a copy of his *Organic Gardening* bible. He took photos and we were in his magazine. "They're not drugged crazed hippies. They don't practice abnormal sexual behavior." How he decided that is marvelous for I heard someone say, "Why I wouldn't go near NY without dope." And he should only (not) know why so and so fled the coop! Oh well!"

Tipi and cook shack

Round Table

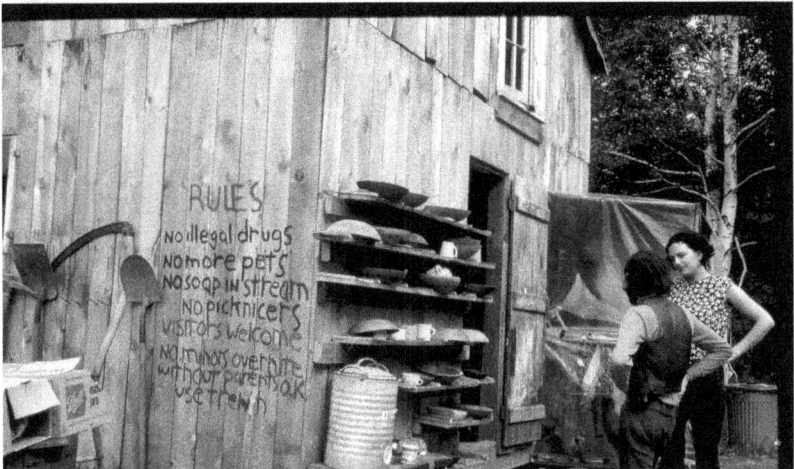

RULES
No illegal drugs
No more pets
No soap in stream
No picknicers
visitors welcome
No minors overnite
without parents o.k.
use trench

Rules and Individual bowls

Rugged Cooks

Skeleton of the long house

Tony in prime seat

Apple truck

Barn entry

Basinette

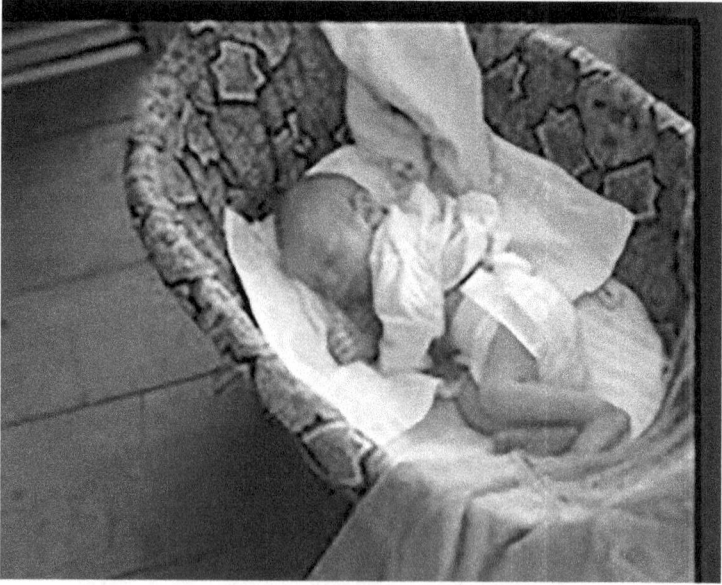

No Nukes baby

Nursing on muleh

Mom, Me, Our Flock

Fred and Nina

Nina and cows

No Nukes Office

Meet the kids

Cordwood piles

Cow Curiouser -Nina's painting

Cow birthing

Cow barn

Out House

Pickle label front

KENTUCKY DILLS

ORGANIC

CRASHING TOWER

PICKLES

32 FL. OZ., 1 QT.
CUCUMBERS, VINEGAR, SALT, WATER, SPICES
DISTRIBUTED BY LLAMA, TOUCAN & CROW
GREENFIELD, MASS.
PACKED BY PHILOSOPHICAL PICKLE CO., WENDELL, MASS.

A PHILOSOPHICAL PICKLE:

CAN WE SAVE OUR ENVIRONMENT ? ? ?

ON FEBRUARY 22, 1974, GEORGE WASHINGTON'S 242ND BIRTHDAY,
A NORTHEAST UTILITIES METEOROLOGICAL TOWER WAS SENT CRASHING
TO THE GROUND ON THE MONTAGUE PLAINS IN NORTH CENTRAL MASS.
TO PROTEST THE LARGEST NUCLEAR POWER FACILITY EVER PROPOSED.

THE TOWER TOPPLER, A YOUNG LOCAL FARMER, TURNED HIM-
SELF IN. HE CLAIMS AS CENTRAL TO HIS ACTION OUR INALIEN-
ABLE RIGHTS TO LIFE, LIBERTY, AND THE PURSUIT OF HAPPINESS
AND THE CONVICTION THAT A JURY OF IMPARTIAL SCIENTISTS
WOULD NEVER AGREE TO DEPLOY HAZARDOUS NUKES AMONGST
THE CIVILIAN POPULACE.

THE 500 FT. TOWER WAS REPLACED IN 2 WEEKS.

MAY OUR CUKES ALWAYS BE NUKELESS

Pickle label back

Turkey sink

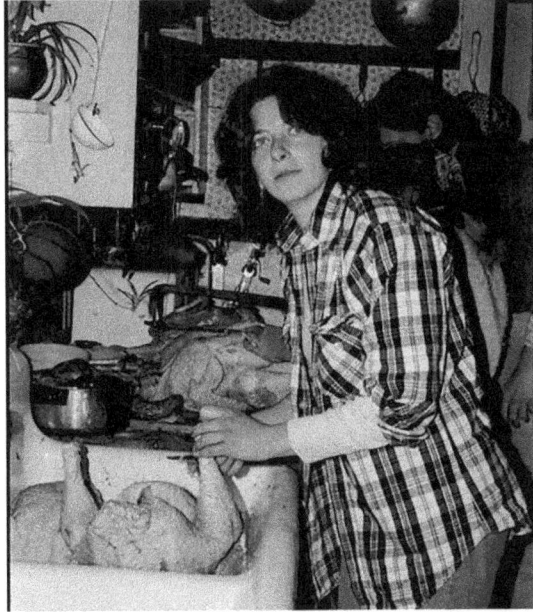

Roofing

Wheel chair barn

Daniel Chainsaw Artist

MARSHALL

Cleaning leads to valuable finds. That was so in two gamey closets, places where reminders of unfinished business did taunt. There were messes of fabric and skewed piles of papers. Failing plaster opened entryways into the internal skeletons of our house. Furtive creatures, galloping yahoos, successfully sought access there for nests. They settled in, gnashed incisors against granite-like black walnut hulls and excreted as rodents do.

I found a bathrobe there. Its history and woolen utility possessed me. Whether it was the wearing of a hand me down, its washed out blending of navy and forest, or the revelation of Marshall's scent, I salvaged it, finger tipping it from piles abandoned after his death. Along with a real typewriter, an unusual cardboard suitcase, fragrant socks and boy magazines, I knew I was attending to a cache no one needed to or wanted to follow to its logical end of a complex identity. All had been crammed in to discharge his room from the terrible sadness of suicide. Someone had closed this door in post mortem resolution, for Marshall was dead, quite dead and no one with heart or energy sorted the mortal lesson from tangible remains. I thumbed the magazines for something of interest in the sheen and application of come hither. Early sex mags had body, youth and luster, but lagged in originality. Marshall had killed himself in the era preceding broader community support. Despite tendencies, there had not been much communication about identity. No one really cared or had to care.

"Oh, those are Marshall's magazines in the hall closet!" and "That's his bathrobe too."

In the wide-ranging society of homosexuals we know today, many had originally been driven by inhibition or justifiably, by fear. The ironic thing was, most of us would have been coolly supportive for we were us, glad when someone found comfort. With minimal focus on sexual ID, it was not a pressing issue. We had read Allen Ginsberg, William Burroughs and The Beats and related flamboyantly. But Marshall's traumatic death and letters highlighted identity issues.

I never intimately knew Marshall. He and Wilton visited the JP for a quick scan and I only remember my sighs as more people came to see who we were and left. I do recall "two tall dark strangers." I picture his face and wild tangle of hair that stood rebelliously distinct. I knew him because I was privy to photos and intimate details. His familiar features might have sat with me in Hebrew school.

In a role of commune clean up lady, when I salvaged his robe, I had not known a spirit resided there. I washed, repaired and wore the asset. It warmed while it itched but was my only robe in that cold house. After years, I ceased to think of its origins and the image from the prized farm photo that showed Marshall in its wrap. Dan recognized it as having belonged to his friend. I remanded it to him. It fit his form better and I did not miss the itch. I moved into another hand me down, this being from my father's Navy days, another itchy woolen heirloom that fit like a rug housing another living spirit.

Marshall's bathrobe draped Dan's body like a boxer on a triumphant march to the ring. He strutted after a bath. His muscles were good. He displayed from the handsome folds of the fabric and came close spreading his wrap and surrounding us. I teased the spirit that established in Dan, but was Dan.

"Marshall, how nice to have you visit."

"You think Marshall would be interested in your ass?" he challenged.

"Male, female, what's the big deal?"

"He preferred male."

"Well, Marshall's pretty happy with both of us right now."

Marshall's Robe

Marshall had been on my mind. Marshall of the dead past, the political, historical Marshall, a powerful usurper of thoughts Marshall, the Marshall I willingly loved despite his absence, despite my never having really known him except once on the fringe when he came to scrutinize The Johnson Pastures. He was significantly embryonic in our extended commune family and because of his strong relationship with Daniel, being both a second brother to him and then, a second untimely dead brother to him. And I'd responded to his face in photos, to his character in stories, the voice in his writing, his active politics and impact on history. He was genealogically familiar to me as ancestors and unborn children.

Daniel and I had been talking about Marshall since files including his journals, letters, thesis and editorials had re–surfaced. A recent and controversial account by an unknown from Marshall's past attributed his suicide to unrequited love.

"I haven't read it yet. I need the right time."

"It won't take long."

But that would not be for it deserved rare uninterrupted attention.

The piece was written about Marshall by a high school associate, an archivist determined to set Marshall's post mortem record straight. This unfamiliar author's insights into Daniel's lost "brother" brought more to bare than Marshall's current friends had concluded. They all knew Marshall was gay. So were Fritz and John and Ray...

"Was he in love with you?"

"He still is."

"Were you in love with him?"

"Of course! I'm in love with us all. Almost!"

The Kitchen and the Closets

You might wonder how we could live successfully with such incongruency of people and styles? To enjoy the intense magnetism of personality, open your eyes, listen and "Swim!"

The countenance of Yankee self-control exemplified while emotions changed but not so much the face. Education varied from Ivy League, to City University and self-educated drop outs. Some of us inherited louder family personalities. Some emerged from uptight separatist suburbia, rugged rural, sophisticated metropolitan. Most of us were diversified middle class with a few blue blood uppers who carried a vestige of importance, deserved or not. There were a few Jews and assorted denominations of Christian. Other major religions, Hindu and Buddhist, were entertained in private practices like meditation, yoga and theoretical consciousness. But practicing religion was not in the fore.

Where we merged was in the kitchen, the center of food and companionship.

Kitchens are a place of action. Ours was an attractive place, for vibrancy, heady aromas and heat assured comfort and familial depth. Our kitchen was a room of beauty that vibrated with farm chores, the energy of our little people, political plots and personal trances. A family that eats together...

Concern for careful cleaning was irregular. It was rare to see a counter uncomplicated. Instead there were lines of unsealed canning jars of pickles, relish, sauerkraut, jelly, syrup, hot sauce, hoi sin, soy sauce, the favored condiments no one felt like cramming unnecessarily into the refrigerator for they were fermentation resistant, stabilized by sugars or maple, salt or vinaigrette.

It took time and interest to rotate or purge out of date oddities, then store clean jars on dank cellar shelves for subsequent canning seasons. There was disinclination or preference about where to plop things. The cupboards were full of assorted tag sale plates hardly termed china but the variety reflected New England. There were too many mugs and dull knives, unless one secreted a favorite. Is this not the way of the world?

Our handmade wooden plank kitchen table seated a dozen comfortably. It stationed steadfastly around the corner from kitchen proper in what had been the Birthing Room with its shallow Count Rumford fireplace designed with beveled sides to radiate heat. The bulky table and the succinctness of the room controlled the space with no footage for other furniture until Peter built enclosed cupboards and shelves.

Not too many of our men noticed boot residue or counter top clutter and some bent stiffly away from housework. Had they lived alone or in a fraternal club, the counters would have contentedly survived under layers while toaster crumbs yearned for release. Instead of unrequited promptings like stamping off deposits at the door or rinsing a dish so gravy not turn to crust, I redirected some of my standards. I was not fanatical but I yearned for more order. My parents had not been extreme. They were more interested in tennis, piano, bridge, reading, and dare I whisper, sex, a formula for a happy life. They lived until 98 years old despite gone by cottage cheese in the recesses of the refrigerator. A nervous relative had scrubbed her counters with bleach to avoid salmonella. Not to be oppressed in the multi dwelling house, I cleaned more than I wanted and tried to ignore the rest. Order made me feel more secure, calmer and allowed time to be creative. This was a communal farm after all. We were American rebels, not American loners.

Perspective had followed me from the JP. Civilizations had survived dirty floors. Women had used cow dung in parts of rural India for ritual scrubbing especially in preparation for sacred festivals.

But there was false pride in casting aside "booger" (bourgeoise) tendencies. Why swab a table to spotless? Why replace everything like Auntie had insisted? Some friends thought it necessary and cool to curse, belch and pick, overt exercises in snubbing one's nose at "the refined." They persisted until their grown children put a stop to attention getting crudeness.

"Booger" this and "booger" that. Pressure to conform sometimes stung when it came from disappointing quarters. After visiting the chicken yard, I washed my bare feet before getting into bed. I valued my booger toes.

A wood cook stove is far different from a wood fired heat stove. It stationed prominently, hot and imposing. It provided serious cooking surface with no fraudulent deceit. It was there to serve, to cook, to heat staked out positions and pots on its broad expanse, one pot boiling up front, another in the center deserving of the magnitude of flame. Side dishes steamed or less insistent ones simmered evenly. Metal frailty was seen at junctures where iron had cringed from decades of fiery force fields upon door hinges. Sensitive corners had crisped away small apertures within which mites of flickering flame were made visible and wavered into the room. That inherited geriatric stove remained precious cast iron, not malleable sheet metal, and with attention supported what we kith and kin did concoct.

Tea drinkers could walk out the door for a handful of volunteer leaves. Freely harvested mint was valued or seen as a voracious garden invader. The blemished stainless steel kettle showed no reflection, just its pulse of boil and breath.

The coffee pot perked suggestive rhythms,

"Come on, come on! Come on. Come on! I want you. I want you. You're so good so good."

Despite the precaution, "a watched pot never boils," committed coffee drinkers held optimistic attention for fresh or ideal temperature, for avoiding the boil of the brew, or stooping resignedly to settle out the dregs. They attentively waited for the right moment to pour or sip, tasting for an unflawed blend.

Floor space was patterned with what no one wanted to relocate into closets had there been one. Just the back room! The kitchen floor remained in its original roughened state where grain swirled with history. I know the founding fathers had sawn and laid but not glossed the wide boards, but I was not yet attentive to hard or soft wood. Wide floorboards and cracks between were the negative shapes of parallel lives. In the kitchen, the hub of activity was immediate so the cracks filled with good soil turned to dirt where corn broom bristles could not reach.

Imperfect sweeping was our culture before we chose to leave crusty shoes at the door for those who exercise the broom and for children who live on floor level. So many times in and out that door. Weary off and on, off and on again, and again and so, what the fuck!

I had not seen Yankee farmer Rob Ripley remove his barn boots in his mud room but I'd not been thinking about that when he ushered me in to greet his ailing wife. Rob thought my simple visit would raise her spirits. "Come! Meet my wife. Let her see who my crew is." She lay in bed, an Ethan Frome figure, the caretaker of his first sick wife, who after her death, married Rob and then fell ill herself. He dutifully tended.

(For the entryway to his Vineyard house, John Abrams constructed a slatted square that topped a shallow hole where boot stomping could effectively deposit, drip or chunk down into an accessible repository.)

Janice's renovations reversed din and soot of muggy walls into cherry wallpaper. Yellow pine floorboards were sanded smooth to reveal the yellowish glow and then protected with multiple coatings to repel caked in treads of unconscious boots.

The original house was built on Chestnut Hill in the late 1790's. There are many Chestnut Hills, for New England was renowned for that deciduous hard wood tree prior to one of our many blights (Dutch Elm for ex) which undermined invaluable wood and nut. Chestnut wood is more resistant to rot than soft woods which are easily scored with a fingernail. Gorgeous yellow pine was suited for floors and finishing work.

The house had three main sections architecturally detectable by inner beam structure and attachment of roofs. The second section was oxen dragged from Shutesbury, perhaps a more economical and resourceful process than purchasing all new supplies and labor.

From the current kitchen, the kitchen had once been stationed in original structure, there were multiple exit or entry ways, doors allowing choices to be made by leading out, up or into. Doors opened into a singular bath tub room with emergency only toilet, a birthing room with its own fireplace, the living room for after dinner tête-à-tête-à-tête-à-tête and music, the porch for mid-day pussycat talk, rocking chairs and porch swing. Above the kitchen were two uninsulated peaked roof rooms only heated by what permeated from below. Another squeaky swinging door led into the backroom, a so-called pantry, used for storage or plop and drop.

What goes on in the pantry stays in the pantry.
Is a pantry a closet?
Come out. Open the doors. It's time to give the closets a good airing.

That unheated chaos of the back room, originally housed living quarters. One ceiling pull string bulb dimly illuminated the accumulation and indiscriminate placement of treasure and trash. Centuries and uneven shifting of sub strata threatened wooden vestiges of old. The single pane double hung windows were currently cracked shut for this was not yet a livable room but functioned for that time.

From backroom level, the tread could lead up a slight rise and into the truly rustic not yet renovated section where collapsed roofing debris now loathed. Once an original living area, it was creatively updated by Fran who retired there with his two sons and then inherited by Peter who renovated further so he could roll up a ramp into his retreat of peace or paramour. A different backroom door led from kitchen to outside. The kitchen attendant at the worn enamel double sink, deep enough to scour the 5 gallon stainless milking bucket, could view the birds, clouds or the comings and goings to the outhouse.

In our house, we were trying to cohabitate peacefully and remain individuals. We were not "Let's have a meeting" type people. We rolled or charged towards goals and accommodated differences best we could. We were a complex and conflicted New Age family. This excerpt from my journal heartens.:

"Lots of laughter downstairs. All the fires are going. What a nice house. Music in the dining room. I could have stayed awake forever so I decided to break the spell and enter the quiet of our room and best of all, to see my baby. To change him, to caress and smile with him. But he wasn't awake, just beginning to stir and he takes a long time stretching, squeaking - thus a nickname Door Mouse. Life is about having a good time. Life is not having a good time. Right now, life is having a good time and being silly with my baby."

BABY BASKET

"Eat more onions. They make you smart!" This was
written in an onion skin paper farm journal one of which
we kept in the outhouse for passing the time, recording or
emergency wipe. Abbie Hoffman's, *Steal This Book*, also
resided there but one unfortunate day fell irretrievably in.

So much revolved around food. None of us was highly
skilled in other than basic hippie cuisine and no one was
heard to complain. When Janice baked brownies, that was
holiday. We ground soybeans and prepared soy burgers
a version of a homemade whopper. Eggplant parmigiana
did not last long enough for leftovers. We relied upon fried
potatoes and onions and "pissy old wheat germ." In Oct. we
were still eating from the garden. Meals invigorated and drew
us towards the long table where the nightly holding of court
brought us close to our shared spirit. This is where the grand
magical appreciation and glamour we recognized in each
other transpired for our brave and reckless willingness to
challenge authority and norms. Little Eben would hold court,
standing high on the bench, finger admonishing us in dictate
to do this or that in animated mimic of those he observed. He
and Quoysters would burst into private laughter.

Blind Fred claimed his fingertip sensitivity partnered
him with dishes, an ideal "blind man's job." Peter revealed
from his wheelchair that loving life included the sink where
he efficiently brought the kitchen to a close. Those two men
added refinery because they congenially abandoned typical
roles.

Sam was the kind of person who could enter the kitchen,
slide what was on the table to the rear, settle his intentions
on the newspaper and enjoy his breakfast. I watched the
intensity with which he consciously followed instincts, eat,
read, get up and go. What was unknown to me were Sam's
multiple connections in the exterior community, some
from academia, Amherst College, U Mass, some within the
networks of farm or mechanics. He charmed and schemed,
understood and initiated much about farm equipment and
procedures. .

Sluggo the historian, was astutely focused on his history

book, *Harvey Wasserman's History of the United States*. He retreated to The Garage to accomplish his academic treatise and then for balance, to field and forest for love of nature. His notorious foray into cooking was an attempt at chocolate chip cornbread. Anna worked in the garden for a few hours in the morning and also the kitchen stirring up woks of rice and beans. She was comfortably familiar with cooking for a large caste yet her tanned forehead suggested much more than farm work but deeper political and environmental networking and research. She knew how to prioritize documentation as she retreated to compile *NO NUKES*, a textbook history of the atom. Tony was a farmer guy planting or tending garden or fruit trees. He would proudly parade into the kitchen his arms laden with harvest, place it on an empty space, grandly smile, and depart. He brought California heritage of orcharding and arrived moments after one of my births displaying a gorgeous platter of sliced fruit. Chuck rather enjoyed splitting cordwood, being in the woods and late-night camaraderie we called "The Owl's Club." Where are they tonight? The Duel, the Maverick, PC? Probably at the Spanish Gardens in "booming" downtown Millers. With a threat of snow in the air, even that would not have stopped a longer transit to convenience a carpool collective.

Grievously unsettling were events that surrounded us like a neighboring fire at "The Ranch." Bad enough to lose everything material, but also Pierre, who ran back in to salvage funds. Later I was informed that his father was a state senator already challenged by his son's renegade activities. That day on our hilltop, I experienced a vague apparition, more so, an impression that zoomed the sky from The Ranch to our hilltop, back and forth zoom and zoom, swish and swipe in great unnerving panic until gone. I did not try to explain it scientifically.

And then Max, Marshall Bloom's orphaned red setter had been found drowned in a cellar well. As with other preceding dogs, the Black Booger with his definingly expressive eyebrows, or was it wooly Shuman the Human, had gone missing, probably to a bullet of no return.

Stevie's anthropological friend Martha, who visited for a short romantic spell, recognized how difficult it must be for so many women to share the same kitchen. In her studies she noted each woman directed her own hearth. I reassured her and ourselves that we were reasonably comfortable, even relieved not having to cook every meal. We did not exhibit harsh possessiveness about space. Over the years and as members changed, friction evolved and expanded beyond the boundaries of the kitchen. Toward the end of the commune days, sharp resentment and newcomer camps formed just like in blood families and the rest of the known world. I was in Wendell by then.

The Art of Language

Farm members were creative with language and coining words.

Dope we called it, joint or le jwan.

"Don't Bogart that joint my friend!"

Very "Soixante-neuf," French for 69, that sexy number we called what was very cool or appealingly eyebrow raising, as well it did sound.

Stevie pasted a notice above our pay phone installed in the dining room after we ripped out the land line for the bill had exceeded feasible. "Loose lips sink ships," he reminded himself, the big talker.

Ped Xing and synchronicity were favorites. We ped-xed, not just as pedestrians crossing, but by taking care of mundane business. This never referred to farm work.

"Who's ped-xing the laundry?" ... or the taxes!

We found correlations between odd events and timing. Sign a guest book in a foreign country and behold there, the name of a friend.

My dad carried the payroll after the Nagasaki bomb onto ships anchored in the harbor, only to learn that his brother, not seen for many war years, had departed on the very same transport that had just deposited him. Ah the heart in that!

Mother of my daughter's friend happened to be sister of a partner with my friend in The Weather Underground.

Ahoy! How we are thrown together!

Because I could not be creative until the coast was clear, I did not enjoy art for years. I attended to our world. It was not until Tony and Peter assisted in partitioning a section in the barn for an art studio, that I focused on myself. A favorite oil painting emerged of the abandoned VW Bug in the barnyard utilized for a pig sty, viewed through a cracked pane in the wooden frame of double hung sash window salvaged from disassembly of the historical Northfield Inn.

NO NUKES

So how did dichotomies meld? When the genius of Sam revealed itself, he could almost do no harm.

In 1973, NU, Northeast Utilities, a mega utility, chose our town in which to erect twin nuclear reactors. I would not call them plants. Another radioactive beast could not be permitted! We tried the obvious interventions: education and leafleting, knocking on doors, speaking at government hearings. A stately electric company official patronizingly patted me on the shoulder and told me, "Don't worry. We'll take care of you!" ("little girl") We organized rallies and marches, opened an office, NICM (Nuclear Information Commune of Montague) and AEC, (not Atomic Energy Commission but Alternative Energy Coalition), formed a political party, NOPE, Nuclear Objectors for a Pure Environment, ran for town offices, and collected 1200 signatures for a state senate district referendum: the majority vote was NO NUKES. The appellation Nuke was spawned around our dinner table.

NU proclaimed the vote was irrelevant and despite the majority anti-nuclear sentiment of town vote, they were proceeding with site plans, surging forward, as well they knew they could. Naturally the citizenry was divided controversially along lines of economics. Tax benefits and jobs in the depressed economy of the area was captivating and many small towns were upended by departure of youths seeking security elsewhere. (We all were seeking!)

Collective trust in government and science and the quest for more energy, spurred others to disparage us and vote for "neighborly" nuclear fission.

"How could you dare to have a child if you believe in the nuclear threat ? How dare you!" one angry proponent of nukes demanded of Sam.

"If you believe in your life style, how can you drive cars and have a tv?"

And

"Aren't you hypocrites for not living in caves?"

Sam called for a house meeting. All attended. He alerted us to his scheme that involved everyone, for he was considering an act of civil disobedience on the Montague Plains, the site where the reactor was planned.

The Montague Plains, Turners Falls, MA, is unique in that it is a geological phenomenon similar to Cape Cod in its sandy aspect. It was formed by the melting and retreating glacial formations which deposited rock and sand terrain, called moraine. Blockage formed Lake Hitchcock 15,000 years ago, the eventual diminution of which shrunk into the great flow "we" call The Connecticut River. The Algonquian language name is "Quinnehtukqut." This river was to be the essential water source to cool the jets of the twin reactors.

On adjoining Montague Plains acreage to the proposed site, the utility had constructed a 500-foot weather tower required by NRC (Nuclear Regulatory Commission) law to compile data: wind, rain, velocity, temperature... for one uninterrupted year prior to licensing of the reactor. Sam's intention was to topple the tower, turn himself in, publicize and expand attention to information, stimulate public relations and news coverage and interrupt the legally required sequence of data collection. He knew the authorities were vigilant about our "boarding house" life style and so could possibly invade us again, confiscate "bastard" children, arrest us for complicity or force us to move.

Since the farm had been invaded by authorities before in seeking cause to harass or ideally, shut us down, Sam's decision would be impacted by group discussion. Would he have proceeded if we had not been unanimously supportive? Interesting question to this day.

That meeting was an emotional and significant moment in our maturation as a tribe. Were we loyally devoted to saving some part of the planet and willing to jeopardize personal standing? These questions philosophically exceeded conflicts of who slept with whom or gastronomical and agrarian values, whether carnivores could span the pasture with barbed wire for meat animals while the vegetarian's basic needs included wandering the hillside unimpeded. Civil Disobedience was on the critical spectrum. The intention of civil disobedience highlighted competitive values: health and survival versus corporate property and governmental policy. Was it essentially responsible to destroy someone's property in protest or to go along with the masses and submit to imposed environmental attack? We all agreed that the nuclear menace outstripped the word of law, so Sam's action, a higher value, attained a status in its own category of legality. A judge and jury would have to decide.

Sam's plan was to slip onto The Montague Plains on George Washington's birthday, Feb. 22, 1974, enact his wonders on the guy wires and turn himself in.

"Father, it was I who cut down the (symbolic) cherry tree."

Sam's actions can be comprehended by watching Lovejoy's Nuclear War[22], a GMP Films production, a farm family film company located on our farms and erstwhile office, BIMS (Bloom Institute of Media Studies) in Turners Falls MA. Personal injury was fundamental to a taut guy wire cable, for when released, it would unpredictably wing around decapitating flora and fauna. Sam, an Amherst College graduate with automotive, physics, mechanical experience and courageous commitment, proved equal to the job. Like other political activists, personal safety did not preempt the threat.

Sam would be forced to prove the necessity of his action in court. He submitted a four page typewritten statement taking "full responsibility for sabotaging that outrageous symbol of a future nuclear power plant." Lovejoy's Nuclear War reveals more of the accounting. His bold action sparked the national anti-nuke movement and instituted changes to our farm and stay at home life style. Sam was renamed The Tower Toppler.

"Hey, does that Tower Toppler live here?"

Sam's trial was terminated due to a technicality and the charges were dismissed due to his being charged incorrectly. He had destroyed "real" as opposed to "personal property."

---

22   Lovejoy's Nuclear War GMP film 1977

Sam's action sparked an international anti-nuclear movement. He became a public figure speaking at national venues and inviting international dignitaries into our lives. A contingent of Japanese atomic bomb survivors arrived, speaking little English but toting admiration and honor for the outspoken hero of nuclear environmental rights. They presented us with small enameled pins with tiny letters proclaiming "No more Hibakusha," the ultimate disaster, relating to persons affected by atomic exposure from the bombings of Hiroshima and Nagasaki.

Where we had gentler notables like Robert Rodale Jr. of organic farming fame visit us before, now we were in the anti-nuclear spotlight. Howard Zinn, Ralph Nader, Randy Kehler, war tax resister (see Daniel Ellsberg,) John Goffman (ex-Atomic Energy Commissioner, author of *Poison Power,*) Wally and Wanita Nelson became household names.

Later when GMP films tackled issues of the Viet Nam war, its impact on the environment (Agent Orange) and on veterans, Bert Pfeiffer, a prominent NAS and AAAS scientist (American Association for the Advancement of Science) challenging the NAS and State Dept herbicide policies in Viet Nam, Country Joe McDonald, my favorite, etc. became familiar figures.[23] Later, in 1979, the five MUSE (Musicians United for Safe Energy) concerts in NY Madison Square Gardens politicized and entertained and our farm community entwined with music stars.[24]

While nuke business dominated, the milk bottles accumulated. The mice raided the squash closet and Jerry Feil, camera man of Peter Brook's film, *Lord of the Flies,* turned his perceptive camera on us. We were animals tending animals, bare and bathing, freshened and feeling good as a wet body can.

The mischievous pigs pressured every fence and pushed barriers. They galloped unimpeded and charged limits of patience. Chase a pig on the lam and forget the insistence of a pressing schedule. Their sneaky smart eyes passionate for release. Clever and neat, John and Yoko we named them,

---

23   GMP films: *Viet Nam Experience, Lovejoy's Nuclear War, Ecocide, The Last Resort*

24   GMP film: *Save the Planet, MUSE Concert, recordings and film*

never soiled their bedding but withdrew to outlying edges to deposit. Tony's orchard stood guardian up the hill. Sam and Janice's blueberry patch reshaped the knoll. Whose goats were they with that terrible stinky billie goat gruff who scared bejesus with his magnitude and horns. The stove slept or changed the temperature. Voices were muffled within private chambers. Books were written, children embraced, themes that typify family life prepared us for the coming day.

Farm life, our loves and tribulations endured, as children, animals, planting, haying and a leaky barn roof continued to compel. Can you picture so many of us worker bees on the 30–40 foot heights of the three tiered barn, dismembering the slate and reroofing the mastodon. John's sister from Australia, Ginny Wilton and I balanced a radio on the peak so as to not miss a day of the Watergate Hearings.

Farm activities were adhesives. And we needed income. The brilliant idea germinated that we grow a huge crop of cucumbers like once before, when Marshall chauffeured the harvest to Oxford Pickles in his Triumph and received piddling for farm labor, This time would not be for pickle company jars but for our own product, Crashing Tower Pickles. Our company was born.

We had become moderately familiar with canning dill pickles and if we had been successful canning over a wood stove, the mass produced challenge did not seem daunting. A difference was the Crashing Tower Pickles would be naturally fermented without the use of heat for sealing. We had little experience in longevity and quality without refrigeration.

Responsibilities were divided. The jobs and lengthy analyses consumed us pleasantly over style, cost, simple glass jars v reusable canning jars, the recipe, manual conveyor belt type sequence and production method, labeling, longevity after picking for maximum crispness, where to sell and how to transport product. Someone sought a large stainless steel work surface and cooling tank, which had been prior dairy implements. And the action began. Oh! Who were the farmers? What field would be used? How fertilized, cultivated and harvested? David Yaghjian, Wendell artist, designed the front label for the jars, a rendering of the tower, crashing of course. A succinct story of resistance, sponsored our

"Philosophical Pickle" was read on the back.

Elation and success sustained for one year. The organic crop was grown at the Wendell farm on what is now a hay field. We worked outside in the L shaped yard protected from sun by sugar maple foliage. Production line assemblage, coordination and camaraderie had some appeal, especially when Charlie Chaplin moderated. The jokesters and pontificators, the organizers and wealth of ideas were rank and file. We actually sold hundreds of jars yet our financial holdings did not swell. Jars were gifted or "went by," though the organic product and recipe were praised and sought.

SEABROOK

After our farm and Sam's environmental renown spread, other anti-nuclear venues became prominent. Our NO NUKES office resounded. Reference files thickened. We were contacted by resistors across country and visited by seacoast anti-nuclear activists. Soon members of our commune began the weekly drive, two plus hours, to help organize against the massive nuclear construction proposed for Seabrook on the southern NH coast. Experience with journalism, public relations and public speaking were comfortable concerns. Liberation News Service at your service!

One Atomic Energy Commission hearing on the coast was held at Wentworth by the Sea. Only a posh hotel could host the notables. I awaited my turn at the microphone while one chair and specific life styles removed, sat a prim, elderly, neatly coiffed lady folded her white gloved DAR hands to present her authority as protector of nature. Public resistance would always be relevant even if not successful. The Clamshell Alliance formed in 1976. The first of several actions were planned. 17 locals crossed onto the site and were arrested.

The second action involved 170 protestors and the third was ten times that again at 1700 willing to challenge the authorities. The skill with which organizers prepared within affinity groups and subcommittees was highlighted: non-violent cd training, safety, media, press releases, creating and printing handouts, legal, medical, communication with police, with participants and with neighbors to determine those who were friendly and would grant us access to their property or phones. Some responsibilities were essential and immediate and some as necessary, for we did not know how long we would be on site or detained: preparing for campsites, toilet facilities, rain gear, tents, medical supplies, food...

Rotations stayed some home to attend to the children and animals. Others regularly drove to the coast and separated into affinity groups, press or organizational areas, or waited at nuke site access points.

Getting arrested for trespassing was something I did not dread. I was white, had resources, community and determination. Three local organizer women invited me to join them in their tent. They were reluctant about who would take the bullhorn to spur North Friendly onto the reactor site. They needed a "spokes." I was a woman from the Montague Farm so it was expected I would have experience. This was unexpected honor. The crowd was expectant. I was handed the bullhorn and inspiration flowed. The backpacks rose and filed in procession to challenge science and government. It was they who were breaking human laws. It was essential to trespass, to take a stand and be heard by press and neighbors about competing harm and options.

Meet the Kids

My child, my darling. My first born. My life. Listen to your child breathe in a dark room. So intimate it nearly breaks your heart.

To describe our farm children is to blend health, energy and bliss, a miso soup candy bar. All the uncles and aunties were smitten with their vivacity and investigative independence. The kids were magnetic but not because of pricy "Oh how adorable!" outfits.

Shopping expenses were disregarded until "No one wears that" and they became adamant about décor. Recently I saw showcased a retro style on a notable athlete, the same simple high top sneakers I bought cheap at Railroad Salvage, like what Eben refused to wear back then.

"I get it now! I get it!"

Little Eben's clothes seemed to just show up and fit well enough with a bit of creative tuck. How nice stripes and patterns looked especially combined with a patch of paramecium to hold the knee together. Polish didn't matter for they played in clean dirt which stained tattoos of freedom.

Cherubic cheeks accentuated Eben's curls. He was a solid figure, strong, resilient and ruddy. His blue eyes, my mother's see-into-you eyes, were clear periwinkles. We did not screech to a halt to wrap him in panicky kisses before assessing damage. Without pandering, he did not develop that prolonged ingratiating overshadowing wail of a crier. He became confident, courageous and secure, not hiding in the folds.

How my sibs had been brought up was:

"Oh you're sick. Go up to bed. Here's a ginger ale. Go sleep it off."

Or

"It's just a little scratch. If you need stitches we'll see tomorrow. It's not so bad!"

And also, the protective, overbearing or dismissive extremes of laissez faire and hierarchy were typical.:

"Don't read in the dark. Come home earlier. Take another sweater." Or "This is not your business!"

In redesigning how to parent, we did as sense made sense. For example, if we were away from home, he would go to sleep where I told him to lie down. He could nestle contentedly on a coat in the corner.

'Neezer' loved our house plants and lectured to a visitor to come see what's growing in our room. "We even have one you can eat, my favorite. Chives."

Young Eben could articulate in sentences. He would stand at our long dining table, "the trough," his pointer finger gesturing along with syllabic directives to listen to this or do that just like an elder.

Sequoya was an enticing sprite with high energy and ragamuffin glee exuding lively naughty innocence. She was long, lean and limber. Quoyster's hands were in motion as if she received synoptic messages she inscribed in the air. Her fingers were lit with motion and art. She made music unconsciously in those spread out fingers with sounds and expressive hand gestures in double time, a twice over way to communicate. Her curiosity wanted what Eben had in his room for she was inquisitive and persuasive. Her little dybbuk overturned potted plants, scribbled in the books or led the way to uncork an unsecured visitor's pouch holding what looked like chewable vitamins, "vitoes" not pills but similar in shape. I can't picture the scene, how Eben, the younger by six months and with a different nature, followed, but he did not need his stomach pumped. With each other, they diverged, asserted, dominated, ignored and loved like new age siblings.

Janice constructed a wooden two-seater high chair onto the wall. The kids sat side by side chomping, smearing enjoying their extended family. They learned to eat without painting every surface with "opeemeal" or "meecho choop." They had many of us attentive to their development and emerging language. They lived in Munkamoo (Montague.) With personality and nick names like Neezer and Quoysters, they ruled. My little puppy just called me Daddy!

Eben and Sequoya were not Goodie Two Shoes. They were caught experimenting with matches behind the house! The horror! Still, they had many adoring eyes on them most of the time. My baby never complained for he was a happy boy surrounded by doting adults, which we must have been. Except for a coffee drinker who once spilled her coffee on his head and chastised us for poor parenting.

Very young Sequoya would creep from bed to the sound of someone crinkling a junk food wrapper. "Canty par? Canty par?" she would croon. We admired her acute interpretive sense of hearing. The kids did roam and a neighbor claimed to have seen them down the steep hill to the river at Coughlin's or peddling down to Chapin's variety store on N Leverett Road, a winding paved two-laner. I would never have permitted such wanderings at that young age. But like most kids, they were intent to open their own wrappers. And after scavenging coins in the couch, found someone who gave permission for the excursion. They more so followed instincts and took it upon themselves to go for a jaunt, for permission was without merit or well worth a reprimand.

They had clean-dirt grubby health, and adorable in their patchwork pants, climbed hay bales, understood barn dangers, garden paths, observed animal birth and chugged steamy milk. Our commune kids were attended to with less fear, relatively free from must, don't and shouldn't. There was freedom from pollution, they drank pure well water, consumed organic homegrown everything and were threatened by no menacing avenues. We were not going to oppress our kids as we had been. We inadvertently did something else! Sometimes we presumed someone else was on guard while we tracked our own needs. The kids survived very well as we relied on some socialistic aspects of child rearing. Few sore memories exist in relation to our kids. Like blood uncles and aunties, everyone was affectionate to the kids, responsible and attentive for their safety, specializing in ways the children will remember. Perhaps we should ask them questions about parenting.

The brook was dappled by godly sun spots where there was privacy to just be ourselves. The kids selected flat pebbles to skip, skip, skip or agh, kerplunk. Brilliance of colors. Illumination shifted as the sun progressed. Radiance arced our concealment. We were joyous and reinvigorated by the cold plunge. To hear the kids' shrill gaiety. To see their absolute joy in water. Eben claims he resists our brook today because I traumatized him prematurely in cold water.

Pure running water. Our blessing. Thank you, god. God is everything. Ask a child.

Political actions dominated but the children came first. They were the structure around which farm life centered.

Ill winds did blow. Some hearts grew cold or exploratory and not ready for mono-commitment. Coupling was a conventional practice. Or there was falling in love with passion. Daily commitment, then the nature of the beast unravels, is revealed, even to oneself. Triangles are strong engineering shapes but are romantically unstable.

Love was "just a kiss away." Thank you Rolling Stones, bad boys of 60's rock, who like most of us were unaffected by, even enhanced, by negative publicity. Our Hippie Hilton had cushions, couches and closets. On the other side of the door sat an ex-partner, brooding in a hot spell of kissing away the past.

Retrospectively, I find it unbearable to imagine ever leaving my five year old, choosing to travel and seek sanity by temporarily leaving the farm, the site of unfulfilled partnering.
"Go to Mexico. You have to travel while you can and now you can."
Feeling secure about the care my child would receive, I eventually bought a ticket to fly.

There were responsible others who wanted to care for Eben besides his father. Thank you, Anna and Janice. I asked adult Eben how my departure had affected him and he said it was fine for he was so busy and had many people to be with. Still, I cannot fathom that motherly ache I chose to subdue so I could carry on. But I did when he was five.
"Give me a string bean. I'm a hungry man. A shot gun fired and away I ran." It was when Eben was a grown man and heard Bob Dylan sing this refrain, that he realized my inspirational eat your vegetables chant, was not my own invention.

Much later, ring, ring! "Hello, Mom, I'm in trouble here at school. No you don't have to come and get me. I just have to spend the rest of this week in the rubber room. No it's not really rubber like for crazies. That's a name. It's where I have to go to sit and do work. I just threw a bucket of water on a clown. He'd been spraying the audience with water from a back pack. It was a pep rally with a music group. I just happened to also short out the sound system which ended the concert!"

Proud of my son. What an inheritance. How could he not be creative about injustice?

Jimmy the Kid

Sam thrived in social networks. He devised a plan with neighbors Brentlinger and Ferguson to welcome Jimmy, one of their extra wayward rescue teens, into our community. The lanky obstreperous jaded youth would benefit by our facsimile of family security. He had reading lessons with Anna and this naturally added to his esteem and affections. Jimmy was know-it-all coy and undeceiving as his colors were on display with Nazi paraphernalia and muscles. Years later Jimmy confessed to having merely been pissing us off with corrosive Nazi brashness.

Jimmy the Kid wended his way with antics but especially when he became a willing water carrier. The gravity feed water line from the well, had existed since Ripley's rule. Nine cows sheltered on the dirt floor of the barn. Added to this were three horses Janice spared from freezing elsewhere in an act of animal rescue. Too many large hooved animals vied for dominance. Mid-winter, a dazzling ice palace glazed that cavern, for the faucet had been kicked off and every crevice was sprayed with an icy coating, gorgeous, but goddamn. The only available water source was from our house across the road. Did we carry buckets! Jimmy shouldered much of the load with bravado and manly teenaged pride.

Along Route 47 is a grand Buttonball aka Sycamore tree. I once secreted by its sprawling girth to relieve myself after urgency on the highway.

"Hey! What are you doing there?" boomed a burly voice.

Coming toward me was a beefy cop, arms akimbo, the strut stereotypical. I squeezed and rose and there before me, I recognized Jimmy the Kid, a grown man with two daughters and a wife in the car, his face aglow with prank. "Hey, I recognized you and knew who would be doing that."

In the decades between youth and now, his and ours, Jimmy is still referred to affectionately as Jimmy the Kid despite his maturity, being an active and loving family man, a Teamster, out of work or active, a busy mind, a busy guy. He surprises us by arriving at our door with his manly presence, tall, confident and with intrigue and political shrewdness.

Reasons to be Vegetarian, or Not!

This is my memory. I write this now because of vivid memories and we were intent upon providing as much food as we could while preparing to face the demons of slaughter. The half shell metal barrel steamed hot water over a fire pit for the attentions of butchery. Shrill screams were too human as the pig resisted and was lugged stiff legged to the site. A bullet perfectly positioned, will instantly fell an animal brain dead until the nervous system agrees.

Blood pulsed from the leathery neck and fed the ground, unless someone preferred to collect it for blood pudding. The carcass was inverted, rear legs spread eagled between a notched hunk of wood intent on securing ankle tendons. Then the weight was hoisted to a tree and held at workers' height for gutting, scraping and primitive wash.

The body was stripped of skin, so lurid and bare of hairy bristles, all blood drained by then in the process. The flesh glistened pink with tallow. Separating the sheaths of pale fat made a sharp tacky sound ripping away from muscular adhesions, the place of belonging. How the internals coiled, a gleaming tract of stuffed intestines and greens, still half way chewed were visible between molars and slack tongue, grass to rank exit portal. The mass sloughed away in interactive unitary constancy once meaningfully systematic, once intent on the business of digestion. It smothered itself out of order with a wonder of disengagement from the body cavity into the wheelbarrow. The organs were revealed and vulnerable, moist where they once had been entertained within the protective environment, now disengaged from arteries and veins. This parallel anatomical assemblage emotionally reflected human structure. The vegetarians took a day away from the farm.

Attention rested on the master of ceremony. Sam had been promoted in absentia of any old or experienced farmer, for he had some experience as a teen in farm work. Success depended upon guidance, worker bees, a honed blade and purposeful hands. Dissect between joints, saw or apportion into freezer packaging or cram anaerobically into the wooden barrel thick with rock salt to cure, a correct method we never accomplished.

The meat eaters secured food by husbandry. Grow it, raise it or work elsewhere for cash! Conflict did arise, not over eating habits but over fencing when Sluggo, frustrated by poor communications, threatened to lop the barbed wires that inhibited his free range across the fields.

Men are so hot.

Farm People of Influence, Money, Getting High

Inexperience narrows your mind. You don't even know what you don't know! I did know I did not know enough. I lived with big talkers, influential charismatic story tellers. The Montague collective was composed of analytical, humorous, imaginative, educated people many of whom had historical perspective. Combine those traits with love and there you are at our table.

Sometimes ideas exceeded accomplishments. But if actuality falls short of ambitions, still kind friend, you remain elevated, more so than highness on a polished throne.

Beauty is an easy attribute, indeterminately gifted and then, revoked. But self-confidence, wit and action carried us on.

Someone appeared as a reflection of yourself. That woman, Wonka, had a crew cut. Was it style, a brain operation, women's liberation, the heat? I understood something about individuality when later, I chose to lop off my Joplin long hair to investigate feminine identity and determine the deep complexity of self-esteem.

We children were smug and fell short of ideals. We felt, really felt, short sighted silence of unrealized potential. In this vein, I present our new found family who presided at our table. One tangent lead unsymmetrically elsewhere and eventually back to the main strain. I cared for only so much before silence beckoned. If immersed in my own mind, no one knew or cared.

A common curiosity led to inquiry: "How do you make money to pay your bills?"

Some of us brought private unannounced savings which saved us from having to leave the farm to make money. Some had jobs with a highway department or a school, some were mine-is-yours generous.

"It will appear when needed!" was one of the mantras I never alleged. The bills were paid and there was little discussion or planning for the financial future. Thank you to all who provided monetarily and so too, for those who provided in labor, for time is a source of money.

Nowadays where marijuana is legal within certain social

boundaries, most of our friends do not even puff. Most people I know drink to ease emotional borders. Back then, drugs helped us to pass through time when direction became hazy. They were diversionary, absorbingly fun with lots of talk or they promoted intensity and focus. Getting high distracted when aimless or if one was just lazy. Most of the women did not smoke much, even the now so- called benign marijuana, for we were more health oriented or pregnant, a female mixed bag of intelligence and mis-direction.

Stephen Diamond

Stevie D was a new friend who became a dear relative. He accompanied himself on the guitar and played lovely basic guitar melodies. He filled the room on key. What was it that moved a man to sing in the family room, a welling up of musical emotion about being alive and musically worthy? I was where I wanted to belong when his strumming filled the room. Stephen embodied resistance when he sang an anthem of our times, Bob Dylan's "Masters of War". The lyrics remain acutely relevant. I would wish to include it especially for those unfamiliar or would benefit by revisiting it, yet due to possible legalities of copyright restrictions, I ask you to read those lyrics yourself.

In the tally of his life Stephen was receptive to change, cool in rebellion and quiet with disappointment. His ambulatory and slight frame were reminiscent of Dylan though Stephen was unique. Mysteries vibrated behind him which no one needed to divulge. Stephen was a romantic. Numerous "girl friends" added quaintly to our rugged farm as they unconsciously abused the limited well supply.

He knew how to be a loving farm brother. He was generous and appreciative, bearing gifts of crystals, pendants, retelling escapades, and inventively suggesting how to pay bills. He was fascinated by magic, synchronicity, spirituality, swimming with dolphins, the personality of politics and as intimated, the enchantment of new women. His charm under cool brimmed hats was instantly obvious because it was coupled with amusing insight and intelligence. Ironic humor sounded out with unfettered chortles. His perennial "ciga-joint," was an indicator of "Bad Boy." He was invested with Sagittarian travel lust and maneuvers to finance his style.

Stephen is the well known author of *What the Trees Said*,[25] a personal account of the early commune days, the personages and the notorious LNS heist and relocation from the city. That book, called a cult classic, is read nationally and used in classrooms.

---

25   *What the Trees Said* Stephen Diamond 1971 Delacourt Press

Stephen was a visionary, inventing the concept, the image and the fantasy for an internationally UN sponsored initiative, for the turn of the century Jan 1, 2000 "One Day in Peace" complete with booklet.[26] He sparkled with pure world love bolstered by whorls of possibility. His complicated pursuits later conflicted with loyalty in partnering and fathering. Yet his adoration and awe for his two daughters, Crescent and Maya, was inherent.

Stephen investigated spiritual manifestations on this planet beyond crystals, scepters, mother of pearl, the mental bending of spoons. He struck a relationship with the trance medium, Elwood Babbitt, whose provocative life readings croaked in a voice from another realm, that many participants had in prior lives been famous personages (Robert E Lee, F Scott Fitzgerald). Marshall Bloom too spoke through Elwood's gravelly trance voice in a GMP film, *Voices of Spirit*[27] *suggesting that his death had not been by his hands alone. Stephen called the film a psychic detective story. His reactions when challenged by the pragmatists about his arcane fascinations, ranged from self-deprecation to serious embracing curiosity. He carried a fountain pen and took notes, later writing Panama Red*, a tale of romantic travel and marijuana. Being born in Panama added to his mystique since he was familiar with ex patriots, journalists and shady business.

During the scheming of anti nuclear actions, Stephen was a mastermind of plot and opportunity. He arrived at meetings with outrageous ploys of counter strategies when confronting utility henchmen or NH Gov Meldrim Thomson whose goal was to see us all incarcerated and therefore, stripped of cohesion.[28]

Not everyone could understand or appreciate Stephen's value, his soulful adhesive disposition within community and the positive power of his magnetic force. Substances and profligate self care led to Stephen's demise. I like to think he made a private decision to stop the battle within his poorly nurtured body and that he is now enjoying the spirit that beamed so strongly from behind the veil.

---

26   *One Day of Peace* booklet self published
27   *Voices of Spirit* GMP Films 1978
28   The Last Resort GMP Films 1978

If in expression he was visionary, grateful and filled with adventure, in private he knew guilt. His nervous energy and determination were forceful and he spent his last conscious days in conversation, affections and dare I imagine ironic optimistic laughter with his family (so I hear).

Tony Mathews

Tony was a farm mainstay with homeboy inclination. He was fruitful and joyous, a fierce and friendly war resister and peace lover, a pragmatist who measured income and expense. The clink of the handle and thunk of the brimming stainless steel milk bucket blended with his love of music and lofty themes. Here comes Tony, shuffle scrape shuffle went his slippers. You can hear him singing accurate lyrics on key from across the road or deep in the barn.

Tony's preferred allocation was for fruit trees, field and garden. True to his California upbringing, he planted a New England version of an orchard, up the hill and arrived at one of my births holding a giant celebratory tray of fruit.

Tony opted for fewer dogs, a continual farm challenge, because the ones present were not all wanted. Dogs were expensive especially in the days preceding the environmental logic of neutering.

When the sole barn water source, a gravity fed cistern fed from a dug well way up the hill abutting the border with Ripley was catastrophically drained and frozen, most of us were stymied and negative. Tony optimistically devised how to inspect and perhaps remedy the disaster. We were unsure of burst underground pipes. We lowered a ladder down to the dregs of decay. Dug wells collect decomposition which periodically need to be dredged. His strength could hoist full buckets twenty feet upwards to be emptied while my agility descended. Beyond suggestive snake apertures, I scooped apprehensively into the slough while drips diluted my heady courage. I peered at the speck of tunnel visioning above, Tony's encouraging entreaties a pinhole urging me on. Our work was unrewarded other than by partnership. He was a true embodiment of the best of California. Tony easy going? Depends who you asked.

He was a constant at the farm, a stabilizing presence, directing his energies until he finally surrendered to do something personal, to travel for a few months in Eastern Africa.

Tony brought a darling to live with him. I responded to

Sue Kramer in like manner as to Janice arriving at the JP. Sue was pragmatical, energetic and orderly. She confronted a dim cupboard designating out of date or never to be used cans of this and that. A tin of USDA "meat" malingered there and a can of Susu Bubuk, condensed milk from Indonesia, probably gifted from George upon returning from his two year PhD stint in Sumatra. I nostalgically urged her to salvage the tin and called her Bubuk, a nickname of friendship.

Janice

Janice was central to the farm. She was a "project to completion" person who created beauty everywhere like the welcoming front walkway lined with perennials. She re-plastered the kitchen, erected a large greenhouse, increased the herds. She had to recuperate from the tragedy of Josh's death and re identify herself personally with a baby and with Sam, within a novel dynamic commune. Indoor co-habitation had her yearning for the more ingrained outdoor life of the JP.

The aged plastered walls thinly exposed strips of lathe beneath the crumbles. The room was held together with Janice's wallpapering. If Janice had been remote in the morning, devoid of a nod or a musical "Good morning!" like Tony, she explained she had been wary of many of us having to negotiate space. Hallways were omniscient, telltale and portentous. But when Janice smiled, oh how she shined. And the sanded floors reflected her toil.

Later she told me, "We didn't have any privacy."
That is how she felt. It was her reality.
The anthropologist would have recorded that fact.
"The walls were so thin. You could hear..."
"Compare that to the JP! No walls! You had Richard's cabin to retreat to."
"Josh never made it that night..."
Wine had been his partner, and then, he was gone.

I reacted to privacy differently for it had less impact on me. With no idea how anyone behaved behind closed doors, there was little information to assess how couples treated each other there, with kindness, consideration or even curiosity. What could be expected from such young people? Maturity might have us caring about and investigating emotions. We were acutely sensitive to private angst and goals and were not so aware of each other's struggles. We had not yet discovered the language of responsive communication.
"How good are we at that now?"
My bedroom had been a haven where a specimen of

privacy and control awaited. The door, opened or closed, was a clear message. As a child in a summer house - nine adults and twelve cousins - I had flourished with noisy exuberance. No cats or dogs but lots of neighbors a skinny alleyway apart and street rumbles off the curb.

Sam

Sam was magnetic, assertive, entertaining, funny and generous. In one word, charismatic like his name. He was keenly incisive with construction, the chain saw and attacking mechanical defeats. With intensity and focus, he would enter a room, cook his eggs and totally engrossed, would settle the morning paper on top of the mess on the table. He knew what was going on in the greater world and where the enemy did thrive to be encountered.

Sam recognized too many left overs. It was rowdy excitement to see him extract from the fridge covered bowls to use down to the scrapings. All went into the large wok. Voila! Sam's goulash. "Dinner is served." How appreciative we were that one of the men controlled the meal. Not to be outdone, he sewed together excess woolen scraps into a patchwork quilt. He drove the sewing machine like a tractor. WHIRRRR, Whirrrr, whirrrr... Did you oil it Sam?

Sam addressed everyone at the table, not just those of consequence. As he talked, his eyes inclusively roved, an uncommonly positive trait. That gift drew people to him and much later, elicited from an adult politician a memory of him as a big person who had entertained her, a child, at the Seabrook antinuclear protest.

He was known throughout the valley even before the tower came down. He chummed with the Rau's's at the gas station, connected us stay-at-homers to other Chestnut Hillers, the Pinardi's, Dave aka Rave Ricardi, Woody Brown at the furniture mill, the Coppingers etc. Because younger Sam had some farm experience in Wilbraham, he was motivated by certain farm projects: haying, silage, fencing and brought the intensity of agriculture home from his labors in Cuba during the time of the Venceramos Brigades, (international sugar cane cutters who went to Cuba to assist in Cuban harvest.)

It was not surprising to witness his Tower Toppler disposition emerge against callous corporate greed and misguided governmental energy policies. We were ready to actively support civil disobedience and stop the reactor despite consequences. We were not followers for despite Sam's initial leadership, there were many roles. We were educated in the science of nuclear reactors. A threat portends, resistance erupts.

Harvey Sluggo Wasserman

Preserving history, protest and devout loyalty to the farm, Sluggo's first rural home, were his protracted and beloved priorities, as were laughter and ridicule of unethical authority. After civil rights and anti-war activities and participating in the 1968 demonstrations at the infamous Chicago National Democratic Convention, Harvey became a journalist for LNS.

Harvey Wasserman's History of the United States is a page turner which presents facts conveniently omitted from traditional high school text about founding fathers and oligarchs. He remained at his typewriter where suggestive sounds emanating from The Garage, were indicative that someone was emphatically at work of the mental kind. Click clack goes the typewriter.

He was a bounteous embracer, full of enthusiasm and romance. "At some time of each girl's life, she has a perfect ass!" He was evidently mischievously profane and crude. ("Every other word is a curse," critiqued my mother.) His offspring eventually would dampen such public pronouncements. Sluggo had outpourings of information and historical anecdote. He was fiercely focused upon his writing be it history or satire. When he was not assembling, cross checking and classifying data or creating outrageous biographical satire about historical figures, the Founding Fathers, high and in love with one another, and with Frenchy, Lafayette, he walked the woods.

Sluggo, an affectionate nickname from his childhood, was sometimes called Squire. Did he not wander the acreage? Maples lined the road and flushed out the sugarbush. Hardwood and evergreen towered above the brambles, daunting even the immodest shrubbery and juniper gin berries, all the growth that thickened the forest. The fields and pastures housed birds differing in habitat and hidden in the under growth, there was real life. He felt the spirit of existence grand in its distinct society.

Sluggo participated in, though he did not initiate large farm enterprise or kitchen prep (except for an inspired time when he baked chocolate chip corn bread.) He loved milking those cows and could be seen a lone figure identifiably musing at natural beauty. "Hey, want me to crack your back?" a homemade chiropractic procedure just to make you feel good. Sluggo connected us to a nearby Kundalini Yoga household and some of us experienced the pleasure pain of passionate rhythmical pounding of our young hearts. He was a respectful vegetarian at table but met his conflictive match with restrictive barbed wire that spanned the pastures curbing freedom to wander. Does this resonate as a farm conflict? I'd say!

Sluggo found it timely and just right to take farm breaks as he was drawn to travel in pursuit of current loves, research, political networking and adventure, for politics was and is his blood. "No Nukes!" "No Nukes to you, Nuk." Nuk was his cold-hearty nickname for me, from Robert Flaherty's book and silent film, *Nanook of the North.* It used to be much colder in Massachusetts and we, like pioneers, braved the newfound intensity of northern weather.

Bob Dylan's lyrics would materialize in random conversation. We were "tangled up in blue," took "shelter from the storm" and knew "a hard rains a-gonna fall." We were genuinely attentive to the on-goings of musical luminaries as young people tend to be. George Sherman was a Dylan aficionado who could recite hundreds of Dylan's lyrics. Freewheelin' Bob Dylan's poetry captivated us as did Emily Dickinson's. Emily (1830-86) resided south of here in Amherst and so Sluggo, incisive and outspoken, campaigned to "Change the Name of Amherst to Emily." The town and esteemed entity of Amherst College were named after Lord Jeffrey Amherst whose alter identity included that of using germ warfare against the "Indians."

"Pass the infected blankets please. It's cold out here. Anyone else?"

Amherst College china depicted mounted British cavalry, swords raised, chasing barely clad Indians around the cups. (Tis true! I uncovered a discarded college cup in a shit pile behind the barn.)

You have to be impressed with power if you shy from challenging it. Sluggo was unphased in confronting blue blood Establishment or any antiquarian relish. Naturally, the excited name change conversation led to considering the same challenge in Turners Falls, named after Captain William Turner who in 1676 led the massacre attack on the native village, Peskeompscut on the Connecticut River.

"We're surrounded by killers. No wonder No Nukes!"

The Green Mountain Post

In the aftermath of Liberation News Service (LNS) press fever, the passion of journalism remained instilled at the core. The spirit of the press continued on with several editions of a farm publication, *The Green Mountain Post*.[29] Stories, poetry, art and photos graced the pages. Readers could join the fun by traveling with Stephen, Raymond and Betsy, or groan at raucous adventures of Sluggo's Thunder Bunny. Johnny photographed pregnant Chuck and me nude for a spoof mag entry, "Name the Baby Contest." Most readers enjoyed the absurdity; a few childish entries arrived. We named the baby ourselves of course, settling on Eben, after Chuck descended from high in the abutting Ripley property. The name Ebeneezer, a Ripley ancestor, struck a mystical chord and so a name was illuminated for our boy.

The name Green Mountain Post evolved into Green Mountain Post Films in 1975 when cameraman Daniel Keller and friends continued birthing various independent films on Viet Nam, veterans, the Nuclear Industry, the arts, peace and assorted documentaries.

---

29 You can view and read about us in *Green Mountain Post*, our collaborative homemade publication after *LNS* and its predecessor, *New Babylon Times* were put to rest. So many of our historical archives have been graciously stored at U Mass. Rob Cox, an archivist of vision, and inspired by Tom Fels, created the resource for us to transplant our books, files and films to the U Mass bunker. Roy Finestone, my father, donated his commune photo collection. Marshall Bloom, LNS, GMP Films, Harvey Wasserman, Anna Gyorgy, Sam Lovejoy, Ray Mungo, Veranda Porch, NO NUKES office materials and other commune members books and documents are collected there. My Nuke and No Spray on the Powerlines files are there too. How enlightening for researchers and my file cupboards!

John Wilton

Johnny was affectionately and irreverently called Sir John because of his stature and heritage -- his father was an Australian diplomat at the UN. John was an engineer of one of New York's bridges. He disdained bourgeoise surroundings and uptight bourgeoise dictates. Rather, he embraced the intrigue and camaraderie of our rural life and the edible commodities more easily obtained. On the farm, he worked across the hall typing *The Green Mountain Post*. As a professional photographer, he presented striking 8x10 black and white images. John's familiar voice welled out now and then like a glob of honey, discussing stories, commenting. His response was wry, his mind so crisp. He rarely discussed personalities, unless there was controversy like too many dogs.

The camps were divided between the dog lovers, the responsible dog lovers, the anarchic dog lovers and those who were non-committal or just didn't like most dogs. John seemed to like, more than like, he loved like children, certain dogs. But the Black Booger was dead and so too dear Quinn. That left Joanie, the queen of dogs, Jasper and the three Anderson dogs who didn't always live at Andersonville but hounded our hospitality and Joanie, our fragrant bitch. Lightening had crashed through the bay window twice seeking protection from the thunder. Because a dog is not wanted, it cowers, snivels and sneaks, irrepressibly obnoxious. Who will tend unwanted animals humanely? Johnny breached the unwanted topic of the five puppies which meant food, love, cleaning the poop, chasing cars. They even had names like Fufu, Stagger Lee, Tank (Atilla). They were getting older and Joanie had weaned them. But no one said The Word. It was revelatory to hear Johnny be adamant. "Get rid of the puppies?" So John, Chuck and Janice intervened and the impasse ended. The pups were offered in Amherst, a town of resource. We anticipated an oppressive mood upon their return. Strangely enough, not so. There was general good humor over grilled cheese.

Anna Gyorgy

Anna arrived at a time when she was seeking personal and political community. Having recently returned from Cuba with the Venceramos Brigade (assisting in the sugar cane harvest in Cuba) she was exuberant to find a place with vitality and organic commitment. She knew how to sharpen a machete and how to wield it. I was pleased with her adaptability to sweaty farm chores and because of this, so to by her beauty which was not shallow. She sought directive about cow barn and chickens so fit neatly into routines. We united over work, weeding our way down the carrot row where conversation did not divert us from finger tipped attentiveness. The farm accommodated her logically, though not with a hammer. She thrived in the kitchen preparing rice and beans sparked by hoisin sauce and her homemade gomasio, ground sesame seeds with sea kelp and soy burgers. When Anna became familiarized with chosen tasks, she announced independence by not needing further advice. She was one of the organizers in our No Nukes storefront office, ran for town office, was interviewed in the GMP *No Nukes* film and was influential in The Clamshell Alliance.

Anna, Janice and I followed Stevie D's initiative to start a restaurant in the Montague Inn which once housed a functional fry-splattered kitchen alongside the barroom. The low ceiling wafted stale beer and no window ventilated where shoulders sat hunched at the bar in display of darker sides. Did we not want to form ties to people beyond our borders? We scrubbed and harvested for serving local bar people and the heretofore unknown parachute club that landed in the field across the road. Wild flower bouquets graced each table where Anna's checkered tablecloths made "diners" feel special. She was the egg roll queen and the sky divers found wonder in our menu of greasy spoon standby and hippie augmentation of farm picked chard salad to health them up.

"Well look at that! The bikers like the greens."
The regulars at Tiny and Ed's Inn soon became familiar with us and anticipated our catering feats.
Stevie D was a willing short order "chef" as he flipped the

burgers and buns, sizzled the dogs and shook the fries. Oh joy! Junk food at the fingertips. Not a lucrative enterprise!

Anna loved tending the kids and she quelled my anxieties about travel for I knew Eben would have an attentive figure in my absence. I see her today reading to any child.

Fred Zapinski

Fred was a political DJ on local UMass radio. He was cool and rhythmic and introduced us to Hawaiian music, especially to Ole Manu. He'd grab a hand and dance us in the kitchen. His refrain was, "Dish washing is a blind man's job." He also made his mark while chopping vegetables with measured care. A true dear friend and attentive to the children, Fred sat them on his lap for stories. Fred was saintly in how he handled losing his vision. He rarely complained about the diabetes that stole his eyes yet remained rebelliously sick of dietary restrictions. He was prone to and profligate with carbs and sweets.

"Hey," he defended narrowly while seeking sympathy as we saw him degenerate. "I grew up with a Polish diet."

Fred's attempt at suicide failed. Sluggo and I traveled to Hawaii to "save" him. His uncontrollable hiccups hurt his ribs. Fred's skepticism denied Polish Peter Tusinski's hiccup remedy, until it worked. He nurtured numerous potted plants on his balcony, the lanai, and fingertipped them to test vitality and wetness. I window sill mature cuttings from his plants 40 years later. Inherited plants recoup people in life.

Peter Natti

His was a happy face no matter the time. Peter was a big man handling a damaged body. He accommodated life from a wheel chair position. Peter's woodworking talents were highly respected. He maneuvered his chair and body into wondrous angles to mortise, tenon and plane wood into cabinetry, doors or to renovate what was needed. The farm house glowed with a variety of warm wooden hues. His genuine smile reflected an understanding of must, sink or swim, the happy to be alive reality after a compromising car crash. While in training for the decathlon, his passenger seat and so his spine absorbed the impact resulting in loss of nerves waste down, not to walk again. "Beat me with that stinging nettle! More, harder! Ah!" he would paradoxically croon, "Ah does that feel good." He revealed that he loved his life more compared to the machismo of his athletic stardom. Peter too was a great dish washer and a most compassionate friend. He made communal life happier and most agreeable.

Alex Kelly

Alex was the senior citizen of the commune, a raging 40 year elder. He was one of the charms in the house, of British Isle descent and vague military experience. He had worked at Howard Hughes' Spruce Goose plane hangar and so ghosts of a past life lingered.

During my parents' visit, he flirted with my handsome mother, fitted a whitish server's cloth over his forearm and presented hors d'oeuvres on an attractive platter, crackers and pate devised from canned USDA meat paste with a central custard cup of golden mustard. This was offered to her as if in the finest restaurant and my mother daintily flirted back and elegantly accepted his offering, the first non-kosher meat of her life. ("Giggle, giggle!)

Alex fashioned an emotional attraction for Bleachy the blond cat who had been on the farm longer than any other warm blooded creature. Bleachy, common to winter cats, snuck into the house and ingratiated himself by insisting that the dark hallway was his liter. Chuck would toss him out but Bleachy preferred what he preferred. Alex toyed with taking him out west but ... "Ol Bleach in a car!" He flourished in the cradle of Alex's arms. Bleachy was not a eunuch nor so amorous anymore, but was seen clumsy on mounting Mama Kitty. Perhaps cat virility reflected on and imparted energy to Alex, who claimed to be "quite a bed reader." He loved sexy books. His leprechaun gleam rubbed his hands together when he suggested *Tunc* ("Get it?") part of Lawrence Durrell's Alexandrian trilogy.

Alex made noises, ho o o o um, long extended sighs and groans, which further endeared him to me. "Alex," I shouted across the hallway, "God! "Oh Nina, terrible isn't it. I must have been a lion in my last life, a tired lion at that."

He was ok, once more emerging from tentative when he got sick, for he had only one lung and other involvements and unknowns but was denied admittance to the veteran's hospital. Instead he was plied with pain, tension and anti-pills as a special British Isle remedy. Alex had pills for everything and would administer or offer "One or two - if you like!" There was a radio in his room. He had been a prime news caster, interpreter and story teller, reporting for our pleasure incoming details of our generation. "You'll never guess who's wanted for murder or who's escaped from jail? The Weathermen, Timothy Leary. There was an unnecessary train wreck, revenge killings..." his voice emanated from any room. "This Black militant just said he used to be non-violent, but not anymore." Anything that blew the norm, from revolution to molestation, Alex reported it all. He once was a radio man on a ship and on an airplane too. That explains it!

Alex was one of my darlings, mellow and aware to not pursue more than one intimate brotherly night. When he disintegrated into society away from the farm, I could not accept his ties were thin, but rather mysterious. As he did not communicate further, complicated history was suggested. I miss him more than I like with unfinished affections.

Albert Maioletesi

Albert and Fred arrived at the farm together. They had known each other from where they cabined elsewhere on Chestnut Hill Rd. Albert was a vital studly guy and to his credit, a skilled carpenter. He spent hours helping to reroof the barn and by entertaining the kids. Albert was a welcome sight for he was good and sweet natured, sure enough of himself to add to sap and structure for a short while before the call of independence redirected him.

Fran Koster

Fran lived with us for a few years. He was a gentle man, a father of two young boys and a creative go getter with aspirations to help the planet redirect from destructive fossil choices. He was well known because of his collective masterminding of the Towards Tomorrow Fair at U Mass in 1977. Research and innovations of alternative energy were collected, and optimistically displayed.

Tom Fels

An early resident and friend from Amherst College. I knew him later as accomplished archivist of farm and historical documents. He and his wife, Tully, built a cabin up the hill, an idealistic and separate retreat, a nest for newlies, which was never approved by town zoning and so never fully residential.

Robert J Lurtsema

Every morning during rare alone time in the kitchen, I tuned in to the host of Public Radio classical delight, commentary and paused patience, Robert J Lurtsema. He became a steadfast go to companion and teacher. He soothed, educated and entertained during daily hours of precise selections on "Morning Pro Musica." His was classical college especially when he thematically linked days of programming and played interviews with musicians and lectures by musicologists. If I were dependent upon anyone, it was Robert J for surrounding me with calm and classics. "What will I do without you?" I lamented in advance.

The Outliers

Why refresh bitterness, quite a negative quality? I succinctly revisit the impact of certain farm livers. Passing years have redirected my attention and philosophically eased me forward. Is understanding not superior to bad mouthing? I feel sorry for those who wanted to be included yet lacked something of spirit or inspiration. Some were excessively needy, without contribution or resource. They needed a place to stay and we excited and existed. Some of us did not have emotional surfeit to share. We chose partners so why not house-mates and farm-mates, a form of marriage? Not everyone who solicited us was invited to stay.

Certain Outliers entered the kitchen, rarely to altruistically deep clean. They selected basic ingredients for cooking an infrequent meal, then abandoned clutter and retreated, luxuriating in their participatory accomplishments. If they aspired to wanting to belong as loving teammates, they did not let on. And if they did, then ineptitude displaced them.

Other Friends Our Relatives

Other farm friends were integral to our communal loop as we composed life. Collections of friends include effective leaders, observers, listeners, independent thinkers and doers, quiet ones not instinctually assertive. Remote or unconcealed, all impact the mix.

Betty and Stanley Bell were our senior citizens from Gill, a neighboring town. Betty was a librarian and Stanley a constable, two seemingly straight roles in life. Books and covers! Gentle and yet determined, they became outspoken about the threats of nuclear power despite the resentment of neighbors or friends for their beliefs. They knew they were losing long time friends yet found that void was replaced by young anti nuke activists. They aligned comfortably and environmentally with us socially and at our NO NUKES meetings.

Jim Aron was a well loved friend.
"It's a black Volkswagen! Here comes Jim. It must be dinner time!" What a smile he had, supported by his deep base vocals and twinkling eye. He too was from an academic family and sounded as such. It was not charm but expertise that selected him later to participate in the reconstruction of the Mayflower. The keel, that mainstay without which no ship exists, was one such masterpiece.

Wendell Farm, Wendell Mass

The Duel or Dual, also dubbed Jimmy's Popcorn, was a spoof of a name for the bank account held in common. The name was inspired by the popcorn George bagged for sale at farm band concerts.

Wendell, a nearby sister commune, was where Dan, Iago and Tom shared the deed of the farm after friends graduated from Amherst, Smith, Mount Holyoke Colleges. They were drawn to rural life in the alluring CT Valley of their college days where friendships were fortified in dorm and class and with Marshall Bloom at the nearby Montague Farm.

The collection of like enough minded friends was subtitled subordinately yet with underlying implications, The Hard Hats v the Artistes. More women lived at The Duel than those living steadily at Montague. I was vaguely curious. Comprehending those I lived with let alone another collection of drop-inners, was time and emotionally consuming. Fond connections were established later. Daniel and I moved from Montague to the Wendell farm to re-establish farm practice and resume ownership from those I unkindly although justly in many cases, dubbed The Human Cockroaches. The eviction tale outrages other stories.

George Sherman

George Sherman was one of the originals, a dear challenging friend, a brilliant and also highly emotional son of Holocaust survivors. There were no fresh socks. Just black matchless interview socks at the side of the hamper. He uninhibitedly pulled, sniffed, smiled and selected.

"Laundry day must be here," he shirked. The socks needed nothing as soon as the shoe was tied. The mound was heaped into his trunk and he thought of it no more, replaced by a trip to Rum's to deliver a stubborn chain saw. George spent no time between thoughts. He chased a runaway tractor down a hill and tried to stop it intellectual style by grabbing a treaded tire.

Then grad school, and PhD. He spent two years in Sumatra with Hedy Bruyns Sherman, (Tripp) working on their anthropological book, *Rice, Rupees, and Ritual: Economy and Society Among the Samosir Batak of Sumatra.*[30]) He met and married Hedy in Singapore, married there and remarried again in the Batak village so the villagers could respect their cohabitation. Hedy was the invaluable glue, the map maker, who provided artist's renditions of agricultural and village life and helped organize data and so, the book.

His room was likewise crowded with the files of an academician researcher with a library and documents on the Holocaust, preparatory for a second book. We were aware of the complexities of being a child of those who "survived" Nazi hell.

I uncovered curious grainy stones in the Wendell garden, one of several similar pieces and asked George what he thought it to be.

"It's not a simple stone. Check the consistency. The Human Cockroaches dumped trash in the garden. It's unidentified residue perhaps from them."

"What do you think it is?"

"It doesn't look like a common stone."

---

30   Dr. D. George Sherman Stanford University Press, Apr 1, 1990

Since I had experienced residual bone fragments from the JP fire, the piece looked familiar with blue burbled texture.

"You think it's human?"

"Well..."

"You think they murdered someone and this is a fragment dumped from the ash can?"

"They're similar to burned bones. Or, could be burned shards of pottery."

George rubbed above the metal pin in his ankle where it ached. He recognized the passing twinge but we found that metal pin when we spread his ashes in that garden. George's untimely death occurred in a fatal crash as he sped his way to Keene State University where he was a professor of anthropology. RIP Dr. G Sherman.[31]

Amherst, Smith, Mount Holyoke College - roommates, graduates and asst. friends

Daniel Keller – intellectual, farmer, filmmaker, prime mover and builder of large farm structures, town government 40+ years

Tom Hoffman, David Yaghjian and Terry Rogers – artists of fame

George Sherman PhD anthropologist[32]

Clare Kittridge, NH journalist

Betsy Corner peace activist and renowned war tax resister

Ira Karasick Harvard Law and much more

Michael Curry, professor

Jim Ord, masterful, mechanical, do all and fixer - compelling energy

Judie Carson Sloane darling of all animals and cheer

Margaret Huffstickler adherent of Adele Davis, brewers yeast, black strap molasses, opera singer, triangle heartbreaker and later on, astounding enough, a white nationalist!

---

31   George Sherman archives bequeathed to Amherst College and a Holocaust Museum in Keene, NH.

32   *Rice, Rupees, Ritual* Economy and Society Among the Samosir Batak of Sumatra 1990

Packer Corners, Guilford, VT

Verandah Porch,[33] one of the original founders, maven of verse, wit, retort, gracious   hostess of grand parties, Guilford Selectboard.

Ray Mungo[34]   author and LNS savant

Fenwick   genius sculptor

Richard Wisanski   professor and Guilford Selectboard for a spell

Peter Gould   fruit tree pruner, author, I grant him grand prize as playwright and actor

Ellen Snyder   Chinese scholar, farm and family

Shoshanna Rhine   ex Weather Underground

Marty Jezer   voluminous author/historian of *Stuttering,* biographies of Abbie Hoffman,
        Rachel Carson, Civil War

Shoshanah Rhin and Marty Jezer, co-writers of an article in <u>Win</u> magazine about how abhorrent criticism may feel. Nevertheless, they propose if one shred of truth or good advice can be plucked from the exchange and considered without defense, then all will not have been in vain.

North Leverett, MA

Susan Maraneck, artist, historical society

Dr. John Anderson, Geriatric Medicine Specialist in Cambridge, MA, hand crafter of wooden bass and cello, still performs and was on Prairie Home Companion

Whit Garberson, lead guitar, peace corps, social worker, kind, kind soul

Willit, NY

Oaks Plimpton, Ira Karasick, Jim Ord, Jarleth- large scale organic farming in the 70's

---

33   Verandah Porch attn to her published poetry collections
34   Ray Mungo *Famous Long Ago* and *Total Loss Farm*

Rhubarb and Old Smokes

When I was a young hippie "chick" on the commune, I had not yet become interested in the locals. It took full attention to raise a child, tend the farm and figure out how to live cooperatively. But the power of curiosity overcame cautious sensitivities of some older gentlemen. They became our visitors. Long hair, no hair! They knew what was inside was not the same as what was out. It could be easier to cope with a stranger than a mate. A stranger can become a friend. Those old guy visitors sparked fascination. They were gentlemen who connected us to the history of our place and so to our own participation in history. They came from the Republic of the Old School, a society revealed by the upheaval of old farm dumps at the periphery of many properties. Spring thaws minutely replicate rumbling origins when aquifers groan, mountains swell, valleys wash wider, high becomes low. Shifting reveals rusted defamed piles of metal and glass but little plastic, an ensemble of life style and material of their times.

"Look! A wheelbarrow, an ancient tractor seat, corked bottles of lumbago remedy."

The sexes are particles that must collide. There flows the glorious tension. Antennae slide up and down; pheromones release. The crook of a lip, the hands. Where had they been and where later? Exchange with these older men within our safe confine, housed no complexity of passion. There was purposeless happy flirtation and friendship emerged.

Those older men found us eccentric and appealing curiosities when they caught us flaunting safety and those oppressive restrictions of their cultures they had grown to theoretically reject. It felt more rebelliously alive for us to occasionally weed in the flesh way down in the garden. We received the sun without care for itch, insects or sunburn on never before sunbathed skin. If we were observed bare, they did not guardedly avert their eyes but continued to smoothly drive on. Charlie was courageous enough to imply and chuckle, his eyes shaded so as not to be indicative of more than "caught in the act."

Charlie, the handsome one, was aware of his smile. He seemed a bit depressed to me. I suspected suspended wild boy humors. Identifying sorrow in a man indicated more depth than he knew how to express. He was not fake, just obscure, and in those days that enhanced his mysterious appeal.

Rob teased, "Oh! Barefoot here too. You only have so many toes. No second teeth on your feet. Watch out for prickers."

Some of us were milking barefoot, having babies without the formality of wedlock, prying with a bar on co-ed roofing, reviving their erstwhile family garden plots, stacking thousands of hay bales high in the massive barn. They were more than willing to advise about farm labors. As older codgers, even beloved chores had become routine and solitary. To be recognized as teachers made them feel important, even more manly. They excelled in natural intelligence, chat about apples, machinery, the weather. How ably they demystified a topic they especially liked, the wonders of animal husbandry.

Rob gently illuminated copulating creatures, great, the cow, and small, all in the missionary position. He was dutifully introducing me to chickens so I could understand that the cock grabbed his henny at the neck, fixated her head down and so raised her rear to sky, the single entry/exit to the reproductive/excretory canal which frequently deposited her bowels, wherever she may be. Shit, piss or egg, all in one composition of function. Upon release from his cockerel ministerial beak, henny would regain composure and vigorously shake herself into feathered order, or deftly flee.

"Oh ho, he's at it again!"

and

"Well look at that. Did you know it's one tunnel to and from? Not like us. Oh no! That's all her systems down there, one shoot. She receives that cock. You'll see it all when you butcher."

and

"Look! There she goes! Finished business! Done! Oh ho, he's at it again! Run! Hee hee hee!"

What stimulus our companionship brought to those older men. They loved the reflection of things past in their romantic memories.

Visiting was a casual time for a Yankee farmer when

they divested themselves of obsessive responsibilities to see what we were up to at the Old Ripley Place. On those visits, there would be buoyant exchange on the porch or at the tilted roadside mailbox, posturing where any of us could enjoy town folk.

The Super C's down.

How's the Farmall doin? Turn any dirt?

The crank surprised me on a back jerk. Nearly took my wrist.

Oh sure! That's the best way to start a machine. No losin the key!

Better the key than your hand.

Knew a fella sayin he could crank it one handed. Easy!

That the fella broke his nose? Too many words in the wrong place.

I figure the plow would still hold to the weld.

Never mind the rocks. Mind the weld.

Nice and easy boys. Nice and easy! And, a good hat.

Robbie Rip

Robbie Rip, known as the "Sugar King" and our sugar guru, was our bordering neighbor. He relied upon us for a bucket carrying maple sugar crew. His own sons had long since moved on so we coordinated with his young grandson, Gary. Rob was easy going, well known and respected in his church where he held rank as deacon. He was a Christian in the high sense of religious moral order as he was non-judgmental and loving. He was "tickled pink" by so many of us uncharted by blood or marriage, living on the farm of his childhood.

Before I identified trees I wondered why we had excluded tapping one large diameter tree.

"Pshaw!" he buckled with glee "Not much tasty sap in that old oak."

"Pshaw back to you!"

He actually said "Pshaw." No one said that in Philadelphia.

Working together motivated mutual consideration. Experience worked the sugar house and newcomers were the collection crews. One season, three of us commune women were depended upon to drive his snowy caterpillar through his family sugar bush and collect the sap. We only encountered two simple mishaps. Getting the crawler stuck meant drawing Rob away from his boiling to chain saw a valuable sugar maple. It embarrassed my heart but he never chastised, so bountiful was his spirit.

Then a driver's mishap had Anna pin me under the wheel of the tractor cart. He leapt onto the driver's seat, instinctively backed off, scooped me up in bridegroom arms, settled me on the couch and sliced off my rubber boot.

"Well I'll be! Just barely blue. Musta been the cushion of the dirt road."

Rob recognized us as fellow soldiers. There was silly awareness in our private agreement to get married next time around. He liked strong women. Grandfatherly hugs were only a bit confusing to feel his chest so near, but his church was the smile of respect and getting the job done. A chortling church man wanted to die singing in the choir and that is what he eventually did at 90.

Stanley Podlenski

I expanded friendship beyond our immediate Ripley neighbor to another Yankee, Stanley the tense one. He was gruff and sour but remained likeable. He had offered me rhubarb roots. His farm on prime flat land of the river valley was visible from the road. The farm house, stiff, white and sharply lined, stood bare as an indication of serious matters and privacy within. No bower obscured; no wild growth demonstrated sensuality. A tight perimeter of lawn was all, beyond which sprawled comfortably, various farm equipment, outdated or functional in a barnyard region, everything in its place, random as it might seem.

I approached the front door and knocked, knocked, knocked. A pause and then the door reluctantly opened and Stanley's wife Ruth stood, not in greeting or curiosity, but in tight disregard and judgment. I had met her twice before. The first time at a market, when upon passing, Stanley, his disappointed mouth suddenly masked by a curt embarrassed "Hello!" and "This my wife; this one of the farm girls." She eeked out a cheap grunting noise. The second time was by invitation, but I had arrived at an inopportune time, their mid-morning donut break, in Ruth's tame, spare and spotless dominion. They were Ruth's donuts and Stanley would not freely offer me one. Christian charity! Manners? Was he inhospitably miserly too in a way I would not know? How those donuts glued and devoured me.

Ruth's grim eyes flicked for a second onto my blouse and what lay untethered beneath. "Well!?"

"Hello Ruth. I've come to see Stanley."

"In the barn!" The door hardly ajar was shut firmly.

"OK! Good! Nothing lost here!"

Now to find Stanley on his farm, somewhere in his man-space. Sun filtered through sideboards, dust showed in rays, a dim atmosphere within a once energized cow barn. Flies buzzed. There was no human motion. I was in a personal space wizened by distance from the time of function.

A further door led me on and I directed my hand to

push. There upon, was revealed a wide low ceiling cow barn and the source of my pursuit. Stanley stood in shock of being observed, a tall man silly in height beneath that low structure. He seemed cowed by having been exposed, for his hand maniacally swiped through the air, a fruitless manual dance to conceal cigarette smoke held low to his head by the interior. Until he focused on me, the intruder.

"Oh, it's you! Thought I'd been caught. Again!"

Did he or I finish his sentence ".... by the old Bag."

Stanley's dry face assumed merriment. An ironic snicker erupted from a mouth not used to the comfort of levity. Relief filled the room. "Ha ha ha! Thought I'd been caught again Here's where I go to have a smoke."

A moment passed.

"Can I have one?"

Stanley turned here, then there. Then near the top of his head he shifted a panel, felt accurately for the concealed pack and we lit up together.

The rhubarb was restive in his overgrown patch where mother plants were dividing. Tobacco and rhubarb were free product. He was tickled to the bone to provide a naive farmer girl one smoky item taboo at his house, the other no longer cherished by his wife or sons who had abandoned farm work.

And then there was another older guy, the dentist, curious about our clan and willing to trade dental cocaine for samples of marijuana. Dr. Pion rhymes with lion, grazes the breast innocently and I am never sure. Oh those old guys born before the generation of free.

Romancing the Air

Revolution and romance did ignite our imaginations. When housemates returned from their travels, we were especially and curiously involved. Steven would suavely enter the room, a coy stranger trailing. There was privacy about exploits but eventually we knew who was important. Some of us carried a starlit aura for we rubbed more than shoulders with actors and politicos. The Muse Concerts in N Y City[35] founded by Sam and Jackson Browne attracted many political activists and allies. GMP Films completed a film for the concert, *Save the Planet*, and environmentally knocked the socks off an audience come to rock and roll. The Peter Brook theater and dance cast brought glamour and intrigue with Helen Mirin et al. Country Joe (MacDonald) and The Fish, Max Gail (Barney Miller) for example were charms.

Jerry Feil[36] was a chum drawn to the promising wonder and theatrics of our lives with his hefty 35-millimeter camera. He valued the most mundane of farm chores, finding film worthy the way we carried buckets barefooted into the barn, or dumped the slops, murmuring as we rubbed the foreheads of John and Yoko, our clean but naughty break out pigs. The garden was highlighted as Tony displayed giant sunflowers and Sluggo strutted proud zucchinis.[37]

Some of us felt sexy. Hippies were reputedly ready and willing, but not necessarily with savoir faire. Most young people are lusty but few were uninhibited or instinctive about giving pleasure. Forget good sex just because you're a hippie. Women's liberation later had us figure out that unsatisfying sex was avoidable. Contented partners expressed what they wanted. That's hard

35   MUSE - Musicians United for Safe Energy. Soon after the Three Mile Island nuclear accident 1979, this anti
nuclear group was founded by musicians and activists inspired by Sam Lovejoy and Jackson Browne: Graham Nash, Bonnie Raitt, John Hall, Bruce Springsteen, James Taylor, Carly Simon, Sweet Honey and the Rock, Gil Scott Heron, Harvey Wasserman and many more.

36   Jerry Feil, film maker and editor of the original *Lord of the Flies* film 1963

37   Why should you lock your porch doors in August? To keep the neighbors from depositing overgrown zucchini boats there!

to do, you exclaim.   How can you say words which sound clinical?

"A little to the left. Not so hard all the time. Now harder! Even more!"

or "I'd like it if you were more aggressive. Try being on top!"

Being passionate does not a great partner make. But unruly passion directed us carelessly.

Not everyone had the fortune to meet a noteworthy director of love. Some of us actually made love, that most intimate and giving between heart, body and soul. Some had sex. Some read novels and learned vicariously, later or never. Shapes, scent and smiles are only some primary bottom lines of attraction. The mysterious magnet of pheromones leaves one in the clouds wondering what has struck so obviously for someone over here but not over there. Yet because people exude pheromones, there is some consolation offered that we all be included. Apple maggots do propel to the pheromone impregnated red sticky ball trap then pathetically lose themselves in the glue.

Scraps Say Get Up

Aside from the debilitating grief of partnering, I was equipped by necessity to take care of needs. Isn't that what women do all over the world? In a sense, I was bi-gendered by doing traditionally manly things like mechanics or driving the tractor. I often arose with my kid in the cold cold and wrestled from smolder, a middling of heat from green wood. I could feel alone in that much inhabited world, except for my child. When he and I retreated to our haven, we could control our energy in the pages of a book or by tending plants. My narrow closet gave purpose with its small order of tools and carton of fabrics. Little man's curious eye spotted how neatly the point of metal sheers fit into the crack on the chopping block and logically, snapped the tip clean off. Those sheers remained functional, connecting scraps into a unified comforter which held us together and beneath which I could focus on his rhythmical breath to fill sleepless time with meaning. Cushioned by the night, the intentions of his compact body were subdued for wee hours where he reinterpreted from life into dreams where chaotic, bizarre colors were eventually understood, to be part imaginative fantasy, part reality.

Get up! I'd say to myself, get up and face the music, song or dissonance. You made choices. You directed yourself, unwittingly to stumble, to fall. Get ready! No crying. Rise up this early eastern window pane. Merge into the happenings of a new day. Despair, disrepair, repair. Life moves on. Get up!

Static thought replaced action and oppressively repeated itself. A sad exchange, an insensitive word and a mood would descend. Tides of frustration would swell and ebb. People were not communicating well, were redirecting priorities, would go their own wounded way, or in and out of love.

"Do I fit in? Do any of us fit in any better, for this commune is not a puzzle with clear edges?" But the farm, the farm, with so much rooted beauty! No taskmaster offers such reciprocal love. The farm, the trees, the moo, the caw, cluck and bleat. In reverse ownership, the farm owns us and tenaciously waits for its caretakers.

Love swelled again in the morning and greeted our new age family who proved to still be there. Oh, here you are again. Someone dear brought in the wood. Thunk! I can hear Tony coming down the hall shuffling his sloppy slippers. Shuffle, shuffle! Or Anna singing or Janice banging dessert pans. Clink and clunk!

Rise Up! Rise up you bum! Rise up and sing how sane you really are. You have all this green buoy around you. It's time. Rise up!

TRAVELS

A big "booger car"[38] drove up, its magnitude absurd, its tail fins slicing the air or slicing through our thighs. CL emerged from the passenger seat. It wasn't such a booger car after all. It was an old gent behind the wheel who had spotted something in the shaggy hitchhiker that rotated his wrists and unlocked his door. Instead of waiting for his wife at church he chose the stranger. He would meet someone new. Yes! He would drive beyond the norm of his paved road and disregard time.

"Where were you? The pastor waited with me for quite some time!" his wife would rebuke. I hope he kept his off-the-beaten-path spirits up.

I await the booger car tale at an expectant door. Where had he been and who the booger car driver? We delivered ourselves from dullness by delving into fantasy, travel or other arms. The comfort of milking and its warm release did not settle emotional turmoil.

I see someone on the hillside. Dusk secured that individual until the aura of intention identified him. Watch your sort-of-partner pick his way up the hill stooping to pluck wildflowers for an encounter. The floral gift wounded more than his divergence, for my hands remained empty. Being a mother with my child, was theoretically replete with identity and comfort, but did not fulfill my soul.

Knock, knock! This at my door. "May I spend the night with you?" The man had shared few personal encouragements before that overture!

"I'm sorry," I squeezed out, embarrassed but able to defend my property.

Why had I not tried a light rebuff?

"Oh you darling. That's very cool you like me. I'm just not doing that now."

Those uninvited suitors were often friends. I didn't want to hurt their feelings because of my disinclination. I had experienced how my inept rejection had determined low

---

38   Booger, a term we assigned to bourgeoise fixation on excessive possessions.

male self-esteem. I cared more for their feelings than my own vagaries. I had allowed what I had not pursued to enter my space where we passed considerately in salty one-sided appreciation.

"Ah, ah ah ah. So sweet. So very sweet."

Or remotely in silence.

Then came a more subtle knock, knock. "May I spend the night?" He was a friend.

One said, "But I don't go the way of women."

Another said, "We're not married. Isn't it good to be with others?"

And the clincher, "How would you feel if I brought so and so to the farm to have my baby?"

Theoretically we agreed. There was no ownership. We were free to discover how to be free.

Crazy! That song! "Crazy for trying and crazy for crying and crazy for loving you." [39]

Couples crashed together, then crashed apart in emotional stalemate. It was true that we were "tangled up in blue."[40] Did we hate feeling crazy? Of course! If you argued the point, you were already going, going, gone. But we were captivated by crazy, the other side of straight which had us wild and free.

Crying hurt too much. It was time to unburden, to control reactions, to acquire self-esteem. The heart wailed. The eyes stayed pragmatically dry. I was thinking about love one way; he thought of it another way and both were conceptually real. I would concentrate on not needing anyone so much.

"She came in through the bathroom window..."[41]

How I liked that image.

---

39   Patsy Cline/Willie Nelson song
40   Bob Dylan's lyrics for that song
41   The Beatles

The window was a door. Objects were not what they seemed.

"He climbed in your bedroom window. Why?"

"You've read Shakespeare. That's why."

He had raised his grinning bare heel over the sill.

"Drama on your doorstep."[42]

On the other side of the door sat an ex, brooding in a hot spell of kissing away the past.

Love was "just a kiss away. We easily splurged with front-line accommodations in our Hippie Hilton for love was possible by opening a door, by sinking onto cushions, into couches. Back then, there were no restrictions. I could leave. But what of our son? Where and how? And we were cementing friendship for when the sex was no longer the point, those most wonderful people remained true to heart and entrusted today.

My crazy brain needed more of me.

---

42   GMP film company motto

Avalanche

The puff
the duchanah
the feathered comforter or quilt
On which culture do you recline
It lies between us
pushed there by hands rejecting heat
or drama
or climactic change
a huge barrier
a mountain range with ravines
a continental divide
of atmospheric
ice age
despite
planetary heat

There is a spell
a force field
we do not breach
divisive boulders resist prodding

Careful and frail we float lofty and groundless in our own
worlds of cool
solitary
blue ether
pushed there
     by psalms,
          a religious order of its own with sound track in
     solo
     by palms as fervently dry as sun
onto stained floors
not only forlorn
but real flat
before the horizon was discovered.

     Despite the complexities, we continued experimenting
and exploring. We rejected stiffening proper this and proper
that. Ironically, one woman, sexually active with my partner,
remonstrated about my sleeping with someone in another

rocky, an even terminated relationship. Her standard, in conjunction with reluctance to communicate further, struck me as fearful, emotionally inept or hypocritical. Suum cuique.[43]

How crushing that all was not right. I was idealistic and optimistic. Feelings were rough and moods didn't easily shed. Bony shoulders jabbed without a hint of humor. Arms redirected attentions and the subtle giggling in the night assumed a different story in the morning.

We were not innocent but carried on with radiant disregard for screwed up possibilities.

"If it doesn't work out, do something else!"

Flagrantly, we directed hungry hearts[44] towards what convinced at that time. Personal relationships continued to impact farm cohesiveness and farm work lost some collective accord as members redirected and accepted work beyond farm basics. As time lapsed, individuals evolved and professional inclinations emerged toward education, music, art, film, medicine, law...

For me, the refrain repeated, "All one's marbles! All one's marbles!" Was I broken?

Crazy whorled my scalp. Centrifugal forces descended behind a sad-sack mouth. No easy smile spread.

There I was rooted in a space called a farm, a place to grow and reciprocate with people and animals. I needed to be resilient for my child. But how would I get stronger for myself?

According to the layers and logic of free love, and according to ways of our exploratory species, I anticipated and accepted what I suspected would unravel. Concurrent with formulaics of balance, and my being on the deficit side of the equal mark, I knew the math of negative numbers.

he + a + b + am + m + e = Minus Me

We preferred crazy to dull. Too upset? Escape into political fervor elsewhere, to the big cities, NY, DC. Nowhere to go? Stay home and confront yourself in this communal life. Or see- saw into silence in the garden or the woods,

<hr>

43   Suum cuique. Latin - philosophical phrase and motto - to each one's own

44   Bruce Springsteen lyric "Everybody's got a hungry heart..."

remembering bright things of the past. Stop brooding. Slow down. Get good and clean dirty.

To see someone's body at the water hole or in private intimacy was more than bare exposure. How one stood and walked expressed their roots of seduction. Not hunched protectively. Not military stiff or chest out boobs. And certainly not in some demeaning suggestive silly pouting butt ass model pose. Not leering at what you have and so "I'm here to get some." But rather "I have something good for you. Do you have something for me?" Now that is sex appeal. The first touch. But we were young and self-protection was not clear.

Four of us allowed Jerry to file us down to the brook to record a cleansing plunge. The historic stone culvert with its keystone construction, backdropped our bodies, its dark eyed tunnel coursed Spaulding Brook to the lower Sawmill River. We appeared a bit stilted before the camera, that outside observer which wanted us natural, but we were not camera practiced. We were bold but not necessarily comfortable, mostly unfazed by nudity in our own lives, or knew we should be because we had shed false inhibitions. Or had we? We did not pursue bare publicity. We did not completely relax nor did we resist the dictates of the cameraman:

Oh, here you are.
This is what you look like.
My camera catches you gorgeous, bare and glistening.
Turn. Jump. Turn.
Click, whirr, shutter snap!

After the glamor receded, paled and was gone, there remained the diapers of life, shoveling, milking, warming the uninsulated house of many wings, all select yet mundane regularities of a cohesive farm. And with us, there malingered the complications of partnering.

We inflict pain upon ourselves and each other. A dear one tries to investigate our inner selves; we might vehemently stiffen, resisting what is native in the other.

There's no exchange for sadness. You might as well sing the blues. There is no choice when there you are and something redirects the feet. Then the equation dissolves; the bond is gone. Too much time spent spiraling, radiating in or out of tightening Fibonacci patterns. My vacillating disposition, stuck me between self-rebuke, weakening of resolve, courage and vision. Or plain old flaming desire.

A darling revealed to me, "You love him more than you do yourself." And with that stark revelation, I was reborn. An invisible forever tie he said we shared, I two-finger snipped us apart. Because of our child, we would be connected for life but we were not inseparable. Such strength, such assertive direction! Until the next stumble and fall. Crazy! Yes! Crazy, but seemingly under control.

It was time to leave for a spell.

Escape to Unexpected

One escape can initiate another. Beware the steppes that from afar appear seamless. Being a homebody with a young son, I was not drawn to travel. I amazed myself when I took the advice of the women at the farm to leave, to trust them to nurture my five year old, to do something for myself and travel because I could. Go to Mexico. Go to Guatemala. See what exists elsewhere. I had never traveled far alone, despite being the wild girl who hitchhiked to Philadelphia with my newborn, a surprise to my family.

I alighted in Merida, Mexico, an English/Spanish dictionary my companion. The taxi driver deposited me at a "hotel" with a subterranean shared room and I flourished for a short stabilization period. My initial morning presented one goal, to locate a place that served oatmeal. That pursuit led me into distant streets and decision making. I was introduced to the cream and crust of flan, preferable to the insufficiently cooked oats.

My self-directed travels unraveled without loneliness. The earthquake that was to come, did not overwhelm highlights of my wanderings.

Intricate Mexican weavings with differentiating regional designs, individually painted homes were indicative of personality so unlike American white wash. Open aired markets excited the senses with piles of moist fruit, produce, clothing, fabric and twine, braided rope and hammocks. Fresh bananas tasted like a different fruit. Over small fires, women deftly flipped tortillas onto flat metal braziers where steamy fragrance puffed. The omnipresent rhythm of patta patta patta patta, patta patta patta fixated attention on a chore so familiar to women, they may not have recognized the musical composition of their ritual or the precision of their palms. It was evidence of women's art and ancestral inheritance.

Narrow alleys were streets with communal water taps. Reserved women intent on their mission hushed and whispering, were shy, disinterested or curious about foreign females. Vast ancient ruins, ruins we flock to photograph and climb, revealed their history. I toted no camera. I traveled light, a philosophical practice, so my mind was my memory. There was wonder and danger in being alone. On the street, "Psssstt, Pussy, come over here, pssstt." Licking their lips, they assumed I would be honored. Psstt, pssssst.

A well traveled friend instructed me to get off a bus in the middle of nowhere if I wanted to meet real people, to walk until I met someone and to inquire if I could spend the night with them. The hospitality at a small bungalow was unique in that there was poverty. Yet the woman, leaning out her unscreened window, invited me in, fed me beans and eggs, aromatic tortillas and showed me where to hang my hammock. She was reserved and I suspect she recognized her comparative deficiency as powerlessness against the odds. I intensified comparisons by the absurdity of my presence. She was bewildered by my being a woman with money to travel and what honorable woman does such things alone and in this fearful country of crime and uncontrollable men on the prowl? We could not speak much for the language barrier was prohibitive but communication was evident when she replaced her common earrings with a pair chosen from my assortment. Her gently enthusiastic son returned from the fields and we poured over dictionaries by a small wick lamp. He looked alike to the mustachioed dignitary on the national stamp he bade me to take so I would not forget his plea for when he would come north where I would be his sponsor. In the night, there was fierce pounding on the woven door. The drunken neighbor insisted he had enough money for the price of me. The woman did her duty as hostess to protect her guest.

Then onwards to the ruins of societies once vibrant, structures some massive and intact, some crumbly. My tourist feet clambered where current inhabitants, wild birds, cawed insistently and unimpressed monkeys flung themselves on viny lanyards tree to tree.

Stolen Guatemalan Goods

Buses spewing diesel trigger memory. They huffed me from Mexico through Belize, a country I did not even know existed and choose not to explore, for rain flooded gutters coursed sewage along and onto walkways.

I boarded a bus towards the small Guatemalan lake town of Flores. The driver maneuvered the cranky, grinding gear shift while his foot avoided gaping holes that revealed the road and where the shaft was essentially attached. His nonchalance was appeasing and I accepted absurdity and my lot.

I shared the ride with chicken crates, kid goats held like babies, nursing mothers, steamy reconciled workers. Young kids clambered on with bowls of tortillas, stuffed leaves, a surprise bit of mystery meat revealed in the corn meal enchilada. They climbed off before the uninterrupted miles between towns. Money making reflected in their expressions, beseeching or pragmatic. Child hawkers participating in family finances and the lure of homemade hot food persuaded me despite the refrain, "Beware the Touristas," that dread intestinal disorder.

I disembarked and entered the first and only open-aired establishment. A concierge behind the counter kept watch over everything, especially newcomers and foreign patrons at her tables. She seemed impervious to extraordinarily bright lights and loud music. The atmosphere suggested that it was "Open For You" by providing inexpensive food and lodging. My speed!

The concierge shrewdly recognized foreign clientele who came and went in her small town. She presided over the hotel desk, estimated duration, who accompanied whom, she predicted escapades and I could tell by the shape of her eyebrows that she raged with stereotyping. She was bound to repetitious sets of experience that limited who she may have been otherwise. She was born, raised and married by predetermined roles. And me, a U.S. hippie who traveled alone was surely advertising myself freely and was either a whore or a whore. The Caucasian hippie men were unappealing to her, hairy and therefore worthless. No need to provide limitless hot water to an undemanding lot. We

were grateful to have a cool trickle and a tightly slung cot.
I was aware of, yet not overly concerned, about contrasting
cultures.

Flores proved valuable in revealing an aspect of
Guatemalan working class, the fear of military power and lake
side simplicity of village life.

One evening, an acquaintance had an irresistible
entreaty. I left my backpack in my unattended room, a room
at first sight, light and airy and later, full of tropical trouble. It
was easy for a thief to enter that room and delve into my un-
lockable army surplus backpack. Especially if one had access
to a room key.

I eventually knew the items were gone for I traveled
light, unencumbered by wardrobe replications, and during
my nightly reorganization, the pocket for minor items was
noted as empty. The invasive fingers I suspected, belonged to
a culprit from a most likely collection of related characters:

The Dour Concierge
Her Proud Rooster of a Son
The Young Fetch-It-Kid.

The stolen paraphernalia had small value except to me
or to someone who owned little:
One - a cheap fountain pen with replaceable cartridges.
Were refills even available in this country?
Two - an insignificant remainder of Mexican coins.
Three - earrings, intended as ready gifts

The disdainful concierge was the most likely suspect.
She perched atop her stool, queen in her fly buzz, bulbs
buzz, busy body bus stop establishment and was central in
her matriarchal show. Arms crossed her chest and tight lips
judged what she could and could not understand or abide.
She had seen me, a kissing fool. She focused on all lodgers
and so, on me, that no bra, singular traveler, puta, gringa, one
in the unending string of long-hairs.

That Guatemalan mother figure, hosted foreigners and
occasional Guatemalan tourists whose national identities
were distinctly observable as they passed through to the

Mayan ruins. She sought profit from any traveler with warm beer and artless yet satisfying enough fare. Her life was to watch, judge and control as she sat in the flickering fluorescence on the matronly iron stool, arms crossed against her heart. This revealing attitude placed her top on the list of suspects.

She recognized longing in the tour guides. Their scant yet actual salary, was augmented by tips. Other professional options were scant, like donning the stiff uniform of the Federales. Young charismatic guides had easy conversation and comfortable grace. They spotted the here today, gone tomorrow hippie chicks. Concierge recognized this one, for he was smooth and oh so very beautiful, a magnet in her rest stop of tacky table tops and harsh illumination. He was not yet subverted by political and social reality and so his radiant axis entertained her tables.

Who was this beautiful young man who proudly displayed an mariposa cleverly stitched on the back panel of his shirt by his revered mother? (mariposa: Spanish for butterfly, possibly related to Virgin Mary, free flight or beauty in nature and in slang, refers to a homosexual.) Was he mariposa or tiburon, shark? Was it his fusion of skin color, the shapes of Castilian and Guatemalan blood lines or the power of his intimacy that attracted?

Foreign girls were eager, unlike her own good girls who went to church, covered themselves properly, wore under garments, had nubias, fiancés if I interpreted correctly, at the proper early age, and saved themselves for their first night.

I did not focus on him nor invent us. I ate my beans, computed the bill and for lack of anything else, gathered my pack to retire. He appeared before me. Basic words in English, nothing memorable, he followed my uncertainty, or directed it away from the lights. I had been loyal to the father of my baby and now in the aftermath of that broken inconvenience, I was free. His presence proved acceptable and soon he enfolded me in arms so lovely, his hair on mine as he whispered, "Primero impacto." How many times before he had seduced linguistically, I did not care, for the breath of those words were true and joined us for one short drifting off and waking again.

He vowed he had never done it before. Too shy he claimed! Ha! The Guatemalan girls just don't! I was easy, white and willing. He claimed no disease and little experience. And soon, he must be up and gone for his early tour guide job was everything to him in his savings for college. We naturally would part. One night only please, the way of travel.

Night had hardly begun, then dawn. He'd return in the morning to those settling into the company's lumbering tour bus as caretaker. He thanked and caressed and held on and was gone. I retraced steps from my venture at his guidebook hotel across the way, up the stairs to the balcony, into my room to ready myself for enduring images and resultant joy. I tramped in, fully engulfed by the night's physical conversation, my hair buzzing with friction and femme. The missing items were neatly elsewhere.

The Senora had cause for jealousy and negative judgement. I was on the road but unlike innumerable men, incurred her judgement. I would be held accountable and would pay.

The concierge had a son. He visited me the next day. She might have watched her clientele but did she know her son? Or had she directed him towards a bounty? Moments before he tapped on my door, I had successfully wrestled a fifteen-year-old go fetch-it kid to the floor. Reputation or my assumed availability had spread. He had come for his portion. Strong enough and marveling at my agility, I won the bout. He left like a wounded dog.

I opened to the next visitor. Do all these guys have a theme? This one was a proud "Yo soy yo!" kind of guy. An actual chest thumper with an identity proclamation that he was himself. In a bit more restrained version of foreplay, he asked, "May I sit? May I hug? May I touch?" and then he was upon me ravenous with the enforced virginity of his caste and rabid with opportunity. The absurdity of being in a second wrestling match with this clumsy, bombastic overconfident young man, cemented confusion. He was not completely repugnant. He was even comprehensible as he entertained himself as if he were a free wheelin' hippie. But he was in an out of sync counter-culture experience and I was not on familiar soil. Adrenalin was horrid and the grim certainty of force froze my immature brain.

Was it rape? If a woman does not want it, even rejects it and then just stops caring and gives up, what is it to be called? He sweetly kissed ears, and held from behind, too inexperienced and insecure to look in the face, not in the ass sex but doggie style. A few virginal pumps it was over and done and he was so grateful and sweet and told about his novia and please be so kind to come and meet her and her family that very day they would be there.

The absurdity of greeting them on my way through the restaurant was keenly amplified as the two families supped at one table and he was so proud to introduce her to me and the girl so sweetly demure with her catholic church scarf and shy smile of fear, expectation, suspicion and innocence.

No wonder the harlot is robbed. In the matron's own establishment where she tenderized theft. She condoned the male, despised the woman. I was lucky in forestalling greater disaster. I moved on.

I needed a bath, a purifying swim in the lake. A kind looking adolescent was lazing on the street and I asked her where I could swim. The young darling stared in amazement for hardly anyone swam. She took me authoritatively by the hand, "Come!" and led me to a relatively deserted waterside place where descending a short embankment I could enter the water. I removed the sundress covering my swim suit and slid into gorgeous water to tangibly change encounters. The youngster stared in wonder, her head in hands on her knees when suddenly, a darkness descended and her face transformed from tranquil bemusement to florid horror. She scrambled ungracefully up the bank to the feet a Federal soldier. He wore his rifle pointing skyward like a sick suggestive message. His chest out, his strut pompous and debilitating, an arrogant dictator of the small, for he had seen flesh revealed and stupid me, I was hardly at the St. Maritz but I was on his turf where women did not disrobe in public. But my amazement increased as I witnessed the transformation of my young hostess to a groveling hair tearing cowed creature, tugging where his trouser cuff dragged the dust. He pondered, closed his fist, chose time to seemingly deliberate and at last pointed away in assent while I'd been struggling to cover my witness back into a reluctantly damp dress. The girl gestured, frantic that I hasten and come. She grabbed my hand and we ran the length of the few houses, turned the corner out of sight of the demon and as safety made us invisible to him, she theatrically became an award winner who winked at me, she winked and clucked her tongue in a sound of ploy for she believed she had out witted an institution. "Vene, come with me to my house. We will be safe." Safe I questioned? Back home in Montague, subservient behavior like hers would have resembled groveling slavery. For her it meant salvation.

And so, I was taken to her home and met the family. Her dad had been mayor so I witnessed the echelon of a non-military official. The entrance to their straight through house led into a spare front room where Mama reclined in her early morning shift. She roused quizzically amused while her daughter explained. Shoulder length hair unraveled to her buttocks in a luminous blast. She swung it around her bare shoulder and reached for a hairbrush. I was treated to the usually private solicitude of her grooming as she put every strand straight and then she was ready. The elder sister, a school teacher, a short and endearing woman in her twenties appeared and we four women, with the facilitation of my dictionary, discussed the world, our lives, my travels, how I could have left my family behind. Without guilting me, they were insatiably curious about sameness and differences.

Are you married? How old are you? Any children? Who is with your child? Why do you not have a round belly? (Cal belly they called it. Cal was the white calcium powder added to whole corn to enhance gluten so as to grind corn into a tacky tortilla making composite, if I understood correctly.)

I was among a family of kind women. Family pain can be excruciating. I did not dwell upon what I did not have, a secure experience at home for my child. His dearest of small faces, was busy elsewhere without me. If my child were to think of me, would I exist on two plains?

Despite the curbs of linguistic limitations, mispronunciation and awkward sentence structures, we enjoyed intimacy.

"And here. Come! See our house. The men are out."

"Yes. I'd like to see how you cook."

"And this, here is our kitchen."

The stove, a two-plate gas burner, a few items on a single shelf.

And then we were giggling and they wanted to learn English curse words. They giggled and covered their mouths in gleeful oh how bad we are and at liberty to be so silly. And they shared what they could with impunity, mother and daughters, and they were uncontrolled for mama had included me in a family joke as she pointed to the line of link sausages strung from a hook. Do you have a word for a long, and she could not say the word, but she directed her hand to her rear and they giggled and coughed their joy at how we were in collusion. She removed the sausages to hold it dangly at her rear. They howled unleashed, jangling not the earrings confiscated by the concierge, but my earrings, relocated from my ears to hers where they belonged in stark contrast against her hair.

In my acute embrace of their worth and honesty, I transmuted and we intersected worlds.

In my travels, there were unanswered perplexities by being on someone else's turf. Who are we as women? How can a traveler leave her child? Will a tour guide be able to achieve an academic goal? Will the Federales persist and subjugation remain? This country exists consecutively on this planet on such different planes. Can the world sustain?

I did not encounter the mayor. The teacher sister hosted me to bat caves and we exchanged addresses so she could find me in America. Another Guatemalan seeking provisions of a better life. Freedom.

From the concise beauty of Flores, I bused on to the sprawling capitol of hardened high rise, Guatemala City. It was easy to find a room near where the bus deposited tourists on a corner or a terminal but most likely in a poorer part of the city. My simplest of rooms was up many stairs and off a central corridor down which I could view ground level a patio where men played cards or a game like dominos. How good to close my thin door, a haven the size of a cell. A confident rap on that door revealed a haughty man who barged in, pistol, wallet and erection in hand to service me while cohorts sat in the atrium loudly enjoying the possibilities. "Yo no quiero nada!" Their jocularity echoed after his rejection when he rejoined the boy's club.

After one day in the bowels of unmarked streets and garbled directions and unhinged by probabilities, I left that city unexplored yet unharmed. Direction led me back to the bus terminal.

My next stop after an arduous bus ride was to Lake Atitlan, where it was suggested, I hike around the lake to remote villages and an authentic Guatemalan experience. I was not enamored with the entry town Panajachel dominated with signs like La Hamburgesa and El Pie Shop. A generous American entrepreneur directed me to use his adobe shack for the night while he paddled cross lake to purchase indigenous items he could sell in the USA.

Ever been awakened by shaking so violent that nothing is up or down, the Earth not where it usually is? My hammock shook one foot up, one foot down. One foot up then one down in furious displacement of body and mind. Flashing lights on the slatted window and screams disoriented and set my mind on fire for the intensity of bedlam was reminiscent of the JP. I was unable to stand or extricate from the mummy sleeping bag. I hopped to the door and out to an empty patio bench. Fear was replaced by subsequent images of decapitation. Ferocious trembling shocks were going to shake the metal roofs already loose, in direct angle toward my neck.

A small camp fire was visible at the adjoining cottage. I approached and came into view where a Mayan family was huddled for comfort, direction and prayer. They were pointing with terror at the no longer sedentary neighborhood volcano which was visibly steaming heat waves from its peak not far across the lake. "Terremoto! Terremoto!" they whispered, as if loud sounds might profane the presence of Earth power or invoke it to further distortions. Terremoto! Earthquake! Terre - the earth, moto - moves. Earthquake! Earthquake! A miniature radio was held to one's ear to hear predictions. A woman turned to eye me, and from the international emotion of being in something together, she beckoned me to sit next to her. Her dark eyes were a peak into Mayan genetics, similarly, a view into the depths of brown eternity. I felt momentarily protected for that family might know where to flee if the volcano erupted. I was included temporarily, clustered around their core of heat. I would survive in the presence of kind though distracted people. They certainly did not need anyone else to care for.

Two Italian speaking boys, other misplaced souls, were also huddled there. Our plans of cashing traveler checks were now thwarted by morning not arriving in its accustomed shape. We decided to climb the road at daylight to Solola, the more populated town at the top of the primitive road to seek a bank. Our climb proved treacherous for boulders, now immovable deposits, were outgrowths along the road. They had obstructed traversing of rescue or escape vehicles. The lake had receded 6 feet with a crevasse opening across and dead fish floating upon the surface. A travel bus had cascaded down the ridge from its perch, yet few deaths had befallen in the lakeside town. We climbed over rocks and observed feats of antiquity as men pried with crude levers at impediments they would not submit to. The careening of those mammoth boulders renewed echoes of the night. After hours of ascent, overhearing earthquake mythology and predictions of renewed aftershock at sundown, we hoped to have enough time to secure funds and return to the lake town. Our possessions and the suddenly comforting American presence, ex-pats and businesses, were there. They would have information and means for escape.

The arrival at Solola was entrance to a form of hell for the zocalo, the town square, was crowded with blanketed bodies, moaning or silent. Commerce was stalled as town energy was focused on survival, not catering to tourists. Word had it that the 7.6 magnitude had incurred more than 22,000 deaths, mainly in the capitol city where high rises had crumbled, and so on. The capitol city I had rejected and vacated mere hours before, had aroused in me a prescient sensation and thus secured my thin grip on survival. The retreat from Solola to Panajachel was more than frenzied descent, for the threat of after-shock loomed and we remained vulnerable twigs on that ruined decline.

In the morning, a talent of competent communicators was able to send the names of American survivors to be listed in US newspapers. They would report to us methods for passage. On the first available bus, I met Sandra and Melodie and we embraced in survivor's companionship.

At a rest stop, we were invited to join Roberto, a self-named American hippie, who drove his van around Central America. He was going to where we were headed, away from the epicenter and towards Mexico. His itinerary included a stop at a natural hot spring. We women wended our way down a steep path while he worked at his van, culturing yogurt in his sleeping bag and toasting granola on a propane stove.

At the bottom, an indigenous family was bathing where icy waters streamed down and intermixed with subterranean boiling waters into temperate bathing pools. This was a secluded family bathing spot and I was struck with apprehension for our intrusion. A woman in a whirlpool summoned me forward to where her family was submerged. Women wore wide bath dresses, the men loose boxer type pants. They all respectfully reached inside to lather and cleanse. The dress I had on made it possible for me to bathe civilized like them while she made room for me to sit. I entered the pool. She offered me her homemade bar of soap. I was renewed and silently marveled.

Suddenly, the bather's eyes refocused onto the path. Horrible! It was bikini clad Roberto descending the slope, a camera in hand to memorialize their libations. We pretended not to know him. They ignored him too as their gentility recorded his lack of embarrassment for him.

We departed from "Roberto" soon after and found a bus to deliver us north to San Cristobal, Mexico. That destination was secured early for I had supposedly been scheduled to encounter friends there according to pre-earthquake plans.

We stayed at a lodging, named something like El Carpenteria, with an agreeable open air center around which simple rooms were tiered. A hot shower was pay as you need, for a fire was kindled with carpentry remnants in the tiny aperture beneath its water cabinet. The carpenters were busy on site and the air redolent with sawed wood.

Sandra wanted to visit her friend, Raymon, a Mexican born in the US, married to an American, born in Mexico, who lived a bus ride away near Villa de las Rosas. They had a dozen or so children. I left a note on the posting board that tourists use, a congealed mass of scrap and letter and directions and pleas, telling my friends my simple plans in case they were to arrive before me. We missed our bus and enjoyed coffee and pastry until we boarded he next trundling bus.

En route, Sandra recognized Raymon's isolated adobe atop a steep hill. We alighted and could soon see Raymon descending to greet his unknown visitors, for the bus rarely stopped below his place. He came closer and closer and I noted that he had the same shape as Daniel. "He looks like Daniel!" And the man, Raymon, came close and climbed over the railing, all smiles and greetings, came to me, to me, and enfolded me. And it was Daniel. He had been on the bus we had missed. Now life had been precarious before that shocker. And however you interpret this, my mind left my body and hovered above the man, Daniel, embracing the woman, Nina, and I could see it clearly from above and then, zoom, I was back in present tense.

We have been together ever since with tree top drama that follows.

What Does Old Mean

What does it mean to be old? My approaching 80 means I am old, yet vestiges of youth persist. Vivid dreams, observing someone's intimate hands, resolving to get lengthy chores or something heavy accomplished before it's too late. A cow chews for hours in grassy sun until she is motivated by need. I do not roam, preferring to stay close to home where the coast is safe, clear and familiar.

"Memom. You say things short. You don't always finish sentences."

I know who understands me by now. I use shorthand in writing and so too in speech. Time is of the essence. We do not know if what remains is a day or a decade. I feed my impatience towards those who dominate the stage, the mic, the air waves. I do not want to hear details about someone's schedule or doctors. "Organ recitals" are necessary between friends.

It is exciting to tell stories of our youth, to herald that young person we were, taking grave risks, yet miraculously evading brutality or early death. If I continue to interest myself, does that mean I am worth living with? What does it take to be a good companion?

The Summer of Love in California, peyote and Owsley's LSD highlighted summer school at Berkeley. Philosophy of the English Language, in which I earned an A on the final exam, was written while high. I signed my name to parachute from a plane. Don't forget to pull the umbilical cord!

But who really cares about the young hippie chick who survived the earthquake and the fire and did not fry. She traveled alone into Mexico and Guatemala and knew nothing of the political climate until grad school when *I Rigoberto Manchu, a Guatemalan Woman* was published. Archbishop Romero was murdered and hundreds of Disappeared Ones were mourned. Then, there and now, on our Native soil, power is defined by taking what it wants.

I brave cold water plunge, but also my family who continues to try to set me straight. Straight is not a line. A line is the shortest distance between two points. Straight is trying not to hurt others. Straight is caring and trying to listen better.

If you learn to speak up not only for yourself, you are going to Heaven. There are no bosses in Heaven. There is no need. There, the rivers are waters to drink. The animals thank each other. Cradle to grave, start to finish is a precept of peace. In Requiescat. Rest in peace. Take time to smell the flowers for you are a human being yet still a twig, a pebble, an ion, a pea, some lint, some frass with memory.

Cock-a-doodle-doo. Hear the rooster?
Then talk, sing opera and tell stories like the hens.

So? Where HAVE All the Hippies Gone?

To know or guess where the hippies have gone is to first know what is meant by being a hippie, a linguistic query. Typical images conjure long hair with little attention to coif. Or inattention to matching colors in what is called an outfit with belt, buckle or tie. There is outward disdain for amassing money yet enough time spent on money for essentials or beyond that, amenities.

Some attribute "hanging out" and laziness as hippie characteristics. We on the farm worked hard. We maneuvered privately around inheritances, bank accounts, jobs, politics and private income. We dealt with what we could afford and purchased little. Some even traveled though not to resorts. A friend resented my calling us hippies, "We are not hippies!" she exhorted. I suspect she referred to that all-encompassing term, to choosing one's own identifying idiom. We identified ourselves by resistance to authority.

Some of us have become professionals or have entered the world of the arts. Some of us figured out how to make enough money to lead lives that do not flagrantly destroy the earth. Some of us are not yet recorded in memory logs We're still here but with different contour.

There was no dictate to becoming a hippie, nor was there a membership drive. We never signed a pledge. Who is on your left or obscured within your core? There you may find a hippie for here we still are. Our hair not so lustrous, our pants not as patched and we can afford to eat more than rice and beans. We have become rich man, poor man, beggar man, thief, doctor, lawyer, wanna be chief.

We acquired skills, became teachers, carpenters, masons, health providers. We built our own houses and some still mow the hay fields. Others appear straighter on the outside, our CPA's who play tennis or ski but remain unconventional thinkers.

Nowadays, the term hippie is not so widely used. People who resist might be called Earth Firsters or -ism-ersters. It was said the hippies dropped out. People still do that by moving away from or towards something like the forest or the mesa. I met a guy who lived on a tiny sail boat and sailed around the seas. I did not think of him as a hippie but rather as an adventuring loner who said ocean life was 97% boredom and the rest sheer terror. Hippies shy from terror. We redirected from dropping away from society to being activists who cared about society and participated in local town government.

Since moving from Montague to Wendell in 1979, there have continued to be environmental assaults that keep us busy. Several were stopped by community action:

> Natural gas and fracked gas pipelines - Kinder Morgan and other corporate giants
>
> Rt 2 stopped from crossing the Millers River and relocating into Wendell Forest
>
> RECONTEK in Orange, MA to burn toxic materials and heavy metals
>
> A car repository in Erving, MA to cover multiple acres above a river
>
> A large scale trash incinerator in Turners Falls, MA
>
> Nestle Corporation's plan to tap into MontaguePlains public water supply for bottling
>
> Turners Falls Airport from leveling a Native American hill, a sacred ceremonial site now registered in the National Register of Historic Places
>
> Preservation of White Ash Swamp Native Burial Grounds

Some threats continue to pose environmental problems:

> Two decommissioned nuclear reactors, Vernon, VT and Rowe, MA that still store tons of highly radioactive nuclear waste
>
> Northfield Mountain Pumped Storage Facility that sucks Connecticut River water up to a mountain repository, killing ecosystems, eroding river banks and using more electricity than it produces.
>
> BESS – Battery Energy Storage Systems using flammable and toxic lithium batteries, clear cutting forests, pouring acres of cement, erecting 30 foot plastic walls to control noise and selling

energy during more expensive peak hours -
energy arbitrage and sending spent lithium
batteries to poor countries.
Aerial chemical sprays for insects or disease that drift
elsewhere into wells, aquifers, public water ways
and organic sites
Sprawl and loss of agricultural land
Toxic sprays on roads and powerlines similar to
or replacements for those used in Viet Nam
Vast solar "farms" on agricultural acreage
The D & B Demolition Debris Dump in Wendell, with
its subterranean fire that burned for more than
a week spewing into the Millers River and which
remains unstable and uncapped.

Content of Character

"Why did you choose him? Why him? Why not me?"
Both are terrible questions of yearning. I chose DW, the guy
who was different from me. How could I not love that man?
He chose to plow instead of attending his college graduation.
How cool and decisive. He knew who he wanted to be. I
chose him because of his smile, the asymmetrical shape of
his mouth and his nose in profile like disdain, but not so.
When he was filming with Jerry in the barn, he concentrated
on the director's emphasis. Later, I knew I could love
DW because he asked my opinion about what should be
recorded. His sharp-eyed camera would present what we
barn people marveled at. He was composed and focused,
brainy and brawny!

Stiffly we resist change. We don't easily clock our own
character flaws even during spiritual moments. Distracting
physical features may actually enhance, like a crook in
a private body part that makes it look as if desire were
pointed elsewhere. Forgetfulness is universal. It is poignant,
humorous and curious yet some of us are unable to laugh
at ourselves. Ha ha, ha ha, ha ha ha! Not so funny when the
saw does nick and who done it?
Is clumsiness significant, as if Big Foot were clomping
through the bed of seedlings, not the foot itself, but
unconsciousness of the plot? Or is an elbow stabbing
your tender ribcage insensitivity? Being unaware of being
unaware is humanly identifying like a lover's insistence, or
needing too much from the wrong person or from someone
incapable of giving your way. Nearing eighty, I begin to
understand neediness and how that sets the stage for losing
oneself.

As we age, curious mannerisms redefine us. Are you
short tempered? Forgetful? The fabulous people who filled
the coffers of our youth may be seen in the present as less
physically attractive yet they maintain glory and worth.
When we have known someone for decades and they
had shown themselves to be of value, then patience and
acceptance are guides. Love conquers all. Oh how I do love

those who are mine!

Those we loved at the farms, after fifty plus years, remain indelibly etched, affiliated like blood relatives. They are tap roots.

I have one regret of my youth with no way to rectify.
"I am sorry," I would be able to say.
We were so young. We were so human. And being human after all, means riptides

Surviving International Collapse

The Ukrainian Church Father cited a parable of a child witnessing religious intolerance, A prophet was being burned alive before the masses and the child repeatedly spit on the flames. "What are you doing child? It will not help!" In reply, the child claimed, "I am doing the best I can."

A Ukrainian woman was killed by sniper fire while collecting rain water. An umbrella was flattened at her side. Uprising endures, but not structure and spoke, those who open their mouths instead of quietly bleating unheard. I open my mother's durable umbrella and feel vulnerable like a peasant beneath the tell-tale jet stream of fighter planes practicing as if strafing the canopy over our tree line on their way to Westover Airforce Base east of here. The umbrella is old and faded but is still a strong umbrella, one she'd acquired when items displayed craft and longevity. Made in the USA and probably purchased at a now defunct department store, it will outlast the obsolescence of collapsible commodity in a society of cheap plastic. Its spokes continue to slide and retract.

What about all the hot spots of fear and hatred? The religious wars and retaliations? The lack of committed international cohesion towards peace and ameliorating climate change?

Take to the woods. The evergreens are umbrellas.

Trees and Religion

Invoking the name of God is not religious imperative. A most obvious spiritual force awaits in the forest where oxygen, natural sounds and peaceful awareness may filter in. Save the forests, plant trees everywhere. Water is life.

Not exactly a tree hugger by stereotype, I investigate an arboreal embrace. I love trees in many ways although not in the hug category. I live with trees surrounding. I select a middle aged trunk that easily fits my embrace and with an open mind, reach out and wrap around. My sensory fingers spread, for there, sap does flow, cells divide in the workings of xylem and phloem. The root mass holds steady and a subtle low key throb rectifies existence. In silence, undistracted by myself, my senses heighten. The tree knows how to live. It simply reaches towards the sun and water below. Mist is absorbed, forces foliage and in what is unrecognized by humans, a relationship of tree colleagues yearns towards tree families. This woody entity, supple or massive, feeds itself. Vegetation alone does grow a mastodon. Unseen minerals make bark and cellulose tangible. The fragrance in the forest is settling and oh so sure a thing. Nature subdues traumatic stress. Hug a tree? While you're there, hug a boulder.

Stevie D wrote his book, *What the Trees Said,* while living at Montague. Stephen was a spiritual guy who knew the right title. Our road, Chestnut Hill Road, where the chestnuts are all but gone, was not ironically named. Both sides now branch over with maple limbs, many planted by the Ripley clan.

Listen to the dripping maple sap at Ripley's sugar house. Approaching the farm house through that tree lined archway is a presentation, a red carpet, nay, a dirt road. A welcoming canopy of boughs and seasonal sap buckets receive you home. Chestnuts once of vast and glorious stature, commodity of food, shelter, industry were blighted indefensibly by what they could not resist. Currently, chestnut saplings in our forest, grow not much larger than a thimble on a finger before they succumb. Researchers and farmers try blight resistant strains and somewhere they persist. And so the name of many a hill, Chestnut Hill, for what once graced the place and remain hand hewn in structures of old.

Eben's young sons sat at our Shabbos dinner table. It was natural that I bring comfort to my son, father of Elijah and Malachi who were being raised to practice Jewish ritual. I directed the pouring of wine, the washing of hands, prayers and slicing of bread. One of the boys nudged his brother for I directed one custom out of sync. I registered their silent mirth. The next day Elijah came to me as I knelt in my garden. He was searching for the others. "Elijah, come here," I entreated. "Welcome to my synagogue."

Am I being political and religious when I take the knee in my garden? Dark knees are clean dirt knees. I take a knee with my god. And yes, connecting to the soil, here is my god, the god of liberty and justice for all.

It is real life when the dark is so thick that no matter how wide you open your eyes there's no illumination. Paramecium poppy seeds of color are in motion behind the eyelids and the spectrum of the brain reverberates. This darkness is glory. This is real and one cannot see the ought to do this or that. None of that lumen from street lamps to ruin privacy of unadulterated darkness. Some people logically fear the dark for there, crazies loom. Some of us prefer dark so solid and dense it fills the room with taste. You can sense it is yourself you fathom, delight and sample.

The golden brook is dappled by transcendent sun spots. There we discern privacy enabling us to be ourselves. The kids select flat pebbles to skip, skip, skip or agh, kerplunk. Brilliant colors, ambers and browns. Illumination shifts. Radiance arcs over disguise. We are as joyous as people can be, reinvigorated by cold repeated plunge, willingly saving ourselves from toil and disease. Pure running water.
Thank you god.
God is everything.
Ask a child.

A Letter Explaining Some Hippie Days

Here is a letter my dad had specifically saved for me. He said wistfully, "Save this. You'll appreciate reading it when you're our age."

I am over that age now. My kids have already proven to be wild intractables. At least no one will easily push them around. My students more than my kids, were more interested in the glamorous 60's. A party theme is to dress "hippie." Clara chastised me for throwing away my bell bottoms. I told her I didn't throw them away. I used them for rags when they fell apart.

Wendell, 1983

Dear Mom and Dad -- You know some of why I left the city. Leaving the city offered alternatives, especially after my divorce required a different starting place.

It's been difficult dealing with me. While you seek normalcy, I can't help but try to escape it. Friends sought our house where mom's baked bread was on the table and dad was curious and welcoming. Remember my Blue Blood friend who claimed his mother was barred in the attic to hide her insane outbursts aka Jane Eyre. Others had parents rarely home. I rejected comfortable materialism while I saw no direction how to counter war and social unrest.

You thought Bob Dylan had a terrible voice but never listened to his words. I listened closely and became a rolling stone. He sure could croon

I had left D Simone, wonderful, talented, sad D Simone. I gave away my house, the van, the furniture. Everything I wanted fit in my little car. Oh the car! I too felt bad buying a German car but it came my way and suited me so I didn't dwell on the conflict. Was that the first German product in our family since the Nazis?

As you know I drove to New England to visit Pamela who was looking for a place to have her baby. That's how I tripped upon the Baby Farm. Instead of her, I stayed.

Hippies were migrating into the country. The locals gagged. Yet most of them moved over if we minded our own damn business. And paid our taxes. Being the most recent newcomers, we were intruders. Of course, the Yankees had forgotten the nature of their own stolen inheritance. The locals, by contrast, were monochromatic. Til you got to know them! Monochromatic and wry, and with determination which prepared them for long winters. They belonged to a society now invaded by a "blooming" culture and I, your daughter, was unconcerned about their existence and claim. Communal life was stressful and cold and took a lot of time to figure out. We had little residential privacy but instead, had farm and woods. We felt spiritually aligned with American Indian's respect for nature. I did not know any Indians other than through books. We responded to the spirit of being pioneers. We wanted "purple mountain's majesty." (Purple by the way was a reference color of LSD) My fruited plains became the hills of Vermont, abandoned farms of Western Mass in the valleys of frustrated revolutionaries. Daniel Shays. And great poets. Frost and Dickinson. We moved into chicken coops and run down Victorian mansions.

Originally, most of us had minimal interaction with and small consciousness of our neighbors as long as they respected our privacy. In return, most of us respected or ignored them and their possessions as separate (but equal) as we patch worked their borders. We claimed public access and public space with rightful power and the indifference white Americans exhibit. In the spirit of the times, we were more than willing to share, while disgusted adults collected belongings, clutched handles on their wide eyed offspring, shooed and lugged and dragged them away from our suspected impurities. Such scenes invariably reduced us to hilarity, for there was a double act of rejection. We were rejecting them, not the individuals, but the corruption they represented and seemed to support. Our towns eventually became integral to our lives and many of us participate in town politics.

We shed birth skins, asserted Constitutional rights to be different. What we could get from the city was becoming irrelevant. Communal life was wildly unpredictable. But we stayed. Today, most of us remain dear friends.

I recognize how courageous of you to follow me to communes. You were curious. I wanted to see you, missing you in the way of a daughter, different from the way you miss a child, but nevertheless, very real.

Dad, you have a vitality with Daniel. You spur each other on to interesting topics and I flourish when I listen.

Mom, you didn't used to like my appearance much did you? I confounded you. But you understood something, were resourceful, resilient and didn't hassle me much. Thank you now for that maturity. We've all matured. Don't you agree? As if aging is cyclical, I'll probably look just like you in a few years. I can see me in you and the kids in us. But those wild days which detached me from you, were great despite the failures. Can parents agree with this? You did well surviving your trials. More to come!

PS   Thank you for the toilet paper!

Green Heals

When I am glum, nature heals. Is that not what I'd always wanted without even knowing? My simplest natural youthful experience had been walks to the city park. There the creek, made insignificant by diverted flow, remained full pungent with spinal meningitis, killed young Eugene Cohen who had waded too fervently.

Trip trap over the bridge. "See that little hole? When I count to three, we all run over and slip through the short cut to the creek where the Billy Goats Gruff live." SCREEEE! A car grazed my leg. I grew up believing what adults said, too innocent to fathom a fairy tale joke.

As a fledgling brownie on a woods trip, I peered at a tree trunk. A spindly legged creature was my secret no one would believe, a 3" flying giraffe. Probably my first uneducated sighting of a praying mantis up close. I secreted that miniscule giraffe into my private stash of protected beliefs. I raised my first hatchet to fuel the camp fire. I chopped and the rebound struck my shin. Pretend and ignore. "Nina! What have you done?" Blood sheened the shape of the slice.

"Oh you vilde chaya!" In Yiddish, wild thing was what I was called.

We abandon childhood honesty for pseudo smiles. My teen years had me drawn to high end cars, not our humble Ramblin Rambler. I wanted to ride his Porche no matter the color. Not yet seduced by green and air, rock, stone, pebble and core, I was moved not to drop out but to drop away from. Then, I found myself on my knees. Greenhorn and green!

A GREEN POEM

July, the usually spare month,
rained so much this year that hoses retired
Watering cans abandoned themselves and
valiant weeds dwarfed the beans
Beetles swam across puddles
like our ridiculous patterns of thought
Green swarms my head
Green too green to be green
Anymore chlorophyll green
will douse the spectrum and the sperm
Hot green
blue grey green
full and fat green
The air floods itself
the eye rests on, settles on, moves away from, flees,
resignedly returns
to the inescapable late August full throttle, log jam green.
We wash stained toes in misty mowed greenery
and green knees speak of kneeling
greenhorns are green
green peas, our green planet
green fractures, green mania, Green Marnier
After dark it is still green out there and when I close my eyes,
green
Ah! shrubs and trees and vines and scrub
stems and stalks and leaves and leaves and leaves
food from the ground to the end of the body is appropriately
tinged green
lettuce, zucchini and greens are green
So my taste buds bellow the nefarious word
and bellow the green refrain
a green blow of green pores and green blood
not blue
but you know what

  In Deuteronomy IX-XX, we are directed to prioritize
and preserve trees even during time of war, especially food
bearing trees, despite the urgency of battle.

I find myself an older woman, climbing the hillside and being at the sunny window. Familiar rocks sprout along the road. If trees are neighbors, you unconsciously salute their presence. I walk the dirt road and see us maintaining hay fields, gentle sloping ravines where cows shelter under scrub elders, choke cherry and viciously spreading yet beautiful multi flora, wild cucumber vines with lawless prickles. Each indent between fields is defined where water seasonally flows creating bog for springtime peepers to serenade the night and each other and savor otherwise scorned weeds to resist erosion.

Celer et Vigorans

Celery says,
   Pick me you fool. I am delicious.
The witch grass responds,
   Try and pick me you fool. I am resistible!
Weeds hold the world together

Who Will

Who will admire my sprawling gardens
And who will tend my flock
Some will notice the clear blue
beyond the soft green of
the black walnut
But who will snip tent caterpillars from those boughs

Who will bum a visitor's cigarette
when my lungs no longer savor fresh air

Who will keep the chaos at bay
that which presses our fences
when posts and beams
do rot and sink and
fall towards natural gravity

After Thoughts

6/23

At the time of writing this paragraph, the international virus scare, reality and/or hype, dominates the news. The airlines, pharmaceutical, chemical, energy, tech companies are being bailed out by government. Isolation on the farm is easy for there is much to occupy us within our community. My teenage grandson said, "None of us will be here in twenty-five years." His current aspiration is to leave the remoteness of the dirt road neighborhood of childhood and figure out what is elsewhere. Relative sequestration on the farm offers a different education. Our grandsons who live on the farm are honing skills: carpentry, work in the woods, cooking, croquet, horseshoes, sugaring, team work, politics, debating, chess, Othello, trampoline gymnastics, political acuity, essay writing and repartee.

5/24

At the time of writing this paragraph, the habitual war in the Middle East weighs heavily upon the international scene. Everyone claims they are for peace. To broker peace and eliminate divisions, respect for differences precedes mediation and certainly reparations. Friends can remember they do not have to agree while they demonstrate respectful listening about history and therefore responsibility. We owe more than following political proclamations from our secure zones.

In Memoriam
Honoring D Simone

D Simone was a man who pursued quality relentlessly. He knew the exact Italian motorcycle he had to have, a Bultaco, the best cameras, Nikons, the ex-queen's house in Germantown, Philadelphia.[45] He was acclaimed by multiple professors at PCA, Philadelphia College of Art, in furniture, camera, sculpture and oils. He recognized excellence in soul music, knew of The Staple Singers and The Apollo Theater (Phila.) where he was one of very few whites in the audience to go see James Brown. He knew how to do the one slide shoe into a room and soulfully sing Duke Duke Duke Duke of Earl Duke Duke...

He was cool and everyone knew it. The ring appeared, he was insistent and in love. Retrospectively, I recognize me, identifiably unconscious, vulnerable and seeking belonging. I redirected yearning for place without confidence or inquiry. Our defects so violently impact others. I do not take responsibility for his suicide. His death letter tried to express his truth. Still, I was a pariah at the funeral, the sea of his suffering family parted so as not to be tainted by my presence. I had loved the man and miss who he would become, but I had not been in love. I express deep sorrow and apologize to his family and to him, an artist, who lost his core and so, his mind.

---

45   I have a handwritten note from Queen Isabella to her agent to purchase a house in Germantown Philadelphia It was found on the wall of that house. I offered it to the Phila. Historical Society and mailed it to them!

INDEX

Who Needs Other Pets

Grandmom's Adoration and Bright Baby Neezer

Identity

The seeds of my personality, as they so simply told us
kids, are not Austro-Hungarian, Belorussian, or Lithuanian
where my grandparents had lived before fleeing. I do relate to
guttural Russian sounds and Hungarian paprika.

There are constant insults to our planet: nukes, chemicals,
herbicides, expansion of power lines, lithium-ion batteries,
corrupt government, greed. But opposing aggressive and
noxious adversaries is not my love.

I live on a productive organic family farm in Wendell,
MA. Some people call me the Flower or Chicken Lady; some
call me Memom. I am calmest on my Capricornian clean dirt
knees.

www.ingramcontent.com/pod-product-compliance
Lightning Source LLC
Chambersburg PA
CBHW071215090426
42736CB00014B/2825